-Utilization Sobriety-

The Body-Mind Link to Substance Abuse Treatment

Bart Walsh, M.S.W.

© 2005 Bart Walsh
Peaceful Pilgrim Press
www.peacefulpilgrim.com

All rights reserved.

No part of this book may be reproduced, translated, stored in a retrieval system, or transmitted, in any form or by any means, electronic, mechanical, photocopying, microfilming, recording, or otherwise, without written permission from the Publisher.

Published in the United States of America

ISBN 0-9755504-1-1

About the Author

Bart Walsh, MSW, is a licensed clinical social worker and Diplomate in Clinical Social Work. Bart has been doing clinical work in the mental health field for the past eighteen years. He has extensive experience in community mental health. Bart currently directs The Milton H. Erickson Institute of Portland and conducts a private practice. He has presented workshops domestically, in Europe and at the invitation of the Milton H. Erickson Foundation. Bart's work has been published in The American Journal of Clinical Hypnosis. His orientation to counseling, psychotherapy and hypnotherapy is essentially a strengths perspective with a solution focus. The strengths perspective helps scan for the resources needed to resolve or modify the concern that is brought to treatment. In his spare time Bart loves to play and compose music.

More information and contact at:
www.affinitycounselingandhypnosis.com

Gratitude

Myriad thanks go to those who inspired and supported the creation of this little book. Thank you attendees at presentations and trainings I've done on *Utilization Sobriety*. Your skepticism and disbelief helped me examine my process and perception more closely. Your referential input and experience taught me much about treatment pitfalls and the power of belief. Your curiosity and daring spirit spoke to an interest others have in a somewhat different, somewhat similar, fail-safe treatment approach to substance abuse. Your enthusiasm and excitement inspired this project.

Thank you people who sought help to change your substance use habits. You taught me how this treatment approach works and how to refine my technique. You bravely provided the raw material from which to construct a personalized treatment. You shared very personal information about experience, wants and needs, in order to explore new possibilities. You inspired innovation and then became a partner in innovation and adventure. I very much appreciate your contribution. You defined the limits common to any treatment. You expressed the possibilities and realized the potentials of the *Utilization Sobriety* method. You helped me better understand what it takes to achieve the delicate balance of maintaining reasonable hope and accepting my own limitations. Thank you.

I have tremendous gratitude for the consistent support, tolerance and encouragement my beautiful wife, Annie McKenzie, has lovingly demonstrated for this project. Annie's eloquent editorial executions were also essential to the final outcome of this book.

Ray Micciche has a talent for seeing the big picture and expressed this talent in his much appreciated editorial remarks. Thank you, Ray.

Kayla Leopold has a well developed sense of theme with remarkably functional attention to detail. Thank you Kayla for your editorial guidance.

Donna Johnson exercised her many skills to provide a clean sweep and overview of this text. Thank you, Donna.

Claire Frederick gifted me and this text with her enthusiasm, wisely tempered sensibility, generosity and tactfully significant suggestions. Thank you, Claire.

Contents

Preface xi

I. The State of Substance Abuse Treatment 1
    Causal perspectives on addiction 4
    Treatment approaches for substance abuse 6
    Level of severity- substance use 10

II. The Evolution of Utilization Sobriety 15
    Case example 15
    Treatment hypothesis 20
    Unconscious communication 21
    State-dependent learning, memory and behavior 22
    The utilization principle 26
    Physiological basis of body-mind communication ... 27
    Principles of body-mind healing 27
    Connecting the pieces 28

III. Source of Strength 31
    Case example 31
    Goal directed strengths perspective and its various
    lenses 32
    The development of inner reality 34
    Personal history lens 41
    Humor lens 41
    Belief lens 42
    Meaning lens 42
    Spiritual relatedness lens 44
    Time orientation lens 44
    Sensory presence lens 45
    Language lens 47
    Choice lens 48
    The problem lens 50

IV. Body-Mind Communication 53
    Case example 53
    Psycho-neuro-somato-sensory network
    communication- our team 56
    Emotional experience and neurophysiology 59
    Genes 61
    State-dependent learning, memory and behavior 62
    Ligands and receptor sites 64
    Psychobiological dynamics with substance- the other
    team 68

V. Evidence of Other Intelligence Within-
    Developing Ideomotor Signals 75
    Case example 75
    Body language- ideomotor signaling defined 77
    Developing ideomotor signals 80
    Variations on ideomotor signals 82
    Ideosensory signals 86

VI. The Utilization Sobriety Method 91
    Eight steps of method 92
    Intention of Utilization Sobriety 94
    Before starting the Utilization Sobriety procedure ...96
    Obtaining a substance use history 97
    Perceived benefits of substance use 99
    A pivotal question 101
    Informing client about access to inner learning 102
    Communicating with the unconscious 104
    The substance-state 104
    The benefit state tool 105
        A negative response to the BST question 107
        Naming the BST 108
        Describing the BST 109
        Other adjustments 111

    Goodbye letter 112
    Withdrawal options 116

VII. Fine Tuning the Benefit State Tool 119
    Adjusting dosage 119
    Regulating duration 121

VIII. Resolving Emotional Obstacles to BST Formation .125
    The Goldfinger method 127
    Goldfinger procedure 129
    Identification and resolution of emotion 132
    Ratification of immediate experience 134
    Cognitive ratification 134
    Imagery ratification- future perspective 137
    Behavioral ratification 138
    Elaboration 140

IX. Sobriety Considerations 145
    Motivation and timing 145
        Curiosity 152
        Physiological factors 153
        Utilization Sobriety influence on
        psychobiological motivation 157
    Sobriety maintenance- relapse recovery 159
    Affect and sobriety 162
    Memory functions 163
    Twelve step peace..166

Epilogue 173

References 179

Index 199

x

Preface

Welcome to this elaboration of a somewhat different approach to substance miss-use treatment. I call this approach *Utilization Sobriety*. The method is simple and easy to learn, even as it encompasses verbal and non-verbal communication to affect a body-mind shift favoring sober choice. This is yet another option for the treatment provider.

This method delivers a fail-safe invitation to rapid sobriety using only the learning within the person desiring change. Because the raw material needed for sobriety is drawn from the client, the term utilization is applied to the title of this treatment. Simply utilizing the client system brings about whatever dynamic changes and benefits unfold. There are prerequisites demanding complicity in order for *Utilization Sobriety* to be successful, as described in Chapter Six. Case examples are presented at the beginning of some chapters.

A brief overview of socio-cultural themes affecting substance use and substance abuse treatment is examined in the first chapter. The current state of substance abuse treatment is acknowledged as a growing, evolving entity, not yet able to comprehensively cry out "victory!" The complex human system demands individualized treatment strategies to increase the rate of successful outcome. *Utilization Sobriety* adds yet another individually tailored treatment option to the mix now available for substance abuse treatment providers. The term substance, as used in this text, will generally reference any drug or alcohol.

The ideas and treatment presented in this text blossomed from seeds planted in me by some generous donors. The contributors are acknowledged for the specific donations they made to *Utilization Sobriety*. Some of the contributions include the premise of *state-dependent memory, learning and behavior,* the utilization principle, the science of receptor site dynamics, the molecular foundation of body-mind communication, a specialized form of body language and integrative synthesis of these concepts. A navigational hypothesis, steering me to the present course, is offered as Chapter Two attempts to sketch out the evolution of this method.

An orientation that applies to my work in general and is at the very foundation of *Utilization Sobriety* is discussed in Chapter Three. Under the guise *Source of Strength*, numerous lenses are presented through which to see and engage a goal directed strengths perspective. This orientation to clinical work typically allows perceived client resistance to be reframed as a strength and integrated into treatment.

The essential body-mind link to substance abuse treatment involves both the structural elements of body-mind communication and the communication itself. Chapter Four focuses on physiological communication in its natural form and in its substance-induced variations. Information about the principal biochemical and physiological players involved with substance use and sobriety are introduced.

Chapter Five extends communication to an operational level. The operation outlines how to employ a particular form of body language to establish a communication system with the unconscious mind. The unconscious can then respond to questions and possibilities very directly. A slight aside demonstrates the utility of unconscious communication through sensory channels.

The first part of this book sets the stage for an examination of the *Utilization Sobriety* method. Following a review of intentions and principles driving the *Utilization Sobriety* approach and conditions restricting its application, each step of the treatment is illustrated with its respective contingencies. Of prime importance is the development of a healthy alternative to using drugs or alcohol. This alternative is called the *benefit state tool*. Withdrawal options are considered in conjunction with using a newly developed benefit state tool. The basic nuts and bolts of implementing *Utilization Sobriety* are in place at this junction.

There are limitless ways to enhance or embellish the *benefit state tool*. Chapter Seven cites only a few useful fine-tuning improvisations intended to idiosyncratically augment the functionality of the *benefit state tool*. This intersection begs therapist and client to creatively consider what custom features might complement the *benefit state tool*.

The majority of people I have seen seeking help to curb or eliminate substance use also need assistance with other themes. Emotional loading is typically quite dense, often as an aftermath of using substance or an initial incentive to start using substance. The emotional debris of the past sometimes poses as an obstacle to the development of the *benefit state tool*. Chapter Eight explores a non-invasive body-mind approach to resolving the emotional past and thereby eliminating emotional obstacles to the *benefit state tool* formation. Application of this emotional clearing process has great merit following the establishment of sobriety as well.

An assortment of practical considerations about sobriety occupies the next chapter. Motivation, as a critical component of most serious change, is deconstructed for examination. Positioning a discourse on motivation at the end of this book may seem a bit ironic since functional treatment can't begin to succeed without motivation. The discussion, however, references elements of the *Utilization Sobriety* procedure that would not be altogether clear prior to reading about *Utilization Sobriety* in Chapter Six. For this reason the elaboration on motivation seemed best positioned in a sequential format. Factors influencing motivation for change and level of motivation are discussed.

Various elements of maintaining sobriety and dealing with relapse are also reviewed in Chapter Nine. Effectively and cautiously dealing with unresolved affect is an important part of maintaining sobriety for many. Unresolved affect involves memory functions and memory functions are quite essential to making *Utilization Sobriety* work successfully. The key role of memory functions colors yet another aspect of body-mind communication. Chapter Nine also explores ways in which *Utilization Sobriety* is compatible with the twelve step model.

The final chapter of this book offers a summary of what has been presented and invites the readers to embellish this method with their own creative, functional adaptations and improvements. The principles upon which *Utilization Sobriety* rests provide a framework receptive to personalized adjustments and additional ornamentation. Integrating a strengths perspective is key to making this approach work well.

Chapter One

The State of Substance Abuse Treatment

*Correction does much, but encouragement does more.
Encouragement after censure is as the sun after a shower.*
Goethe

What if I said you really can experience the best aspects of using whatever substance you commonly use or have used in the past without actually using that substance or any other substance? Hold on to your skepticism, curiosity or whatever this proposition stirs up and read on. This book is about the possibility just raised.

Treatment for the abuse of drugs and alcohol has always posed a formidable challenge to both the treatment provider and the client. The pharmaceutical age we find ourselves in today weaves additional confounding threads into the fabric of substance use perception. Today's social climate is ripe with conflicting messages about drug use. R. D. Laing (1972) suggested it is the proliferation of ambiguous communication delivered by a "healthy" society that complicates psychosis in the psychiatrically fragile in need of consistent models of logical behavior. In spite of inconsistent directives about drug use, advances continue to clarify the biochemical map of substance addiction and to incorporate more of the whole individual into effective treatment.

The messages delivered by much of the public media about moral and political correctness, healthy living and normal human functioning embody a remarkable degree of ambiguity. Of prime concern are the messages about substances that alter psychological and biological functions in humans. Today's commercial media persuasively encourages the for-profit use of various substances to remedy every form of biological, psychological, environmental, developmental or situational distress or discomfort. Billions of dollars are spent annually to promote pharmaceutical solutions to undesirable but normal biological processes. Pills are suggested to enhance gastrointestinal regularity, in place of a good diet and exercise. Affective alteration during the menstrual cycle is challenged with medication. A massive war is being waged pharmaceutically against depression and anything that remotely resembles it. The source of the depression or the personalized meaning it may hold matters not. The immune system is too often insulted by medication before a simple cold can run its course. Alcohol and nicotine use are marketed as pastimes of the young and healthy. The media theme we encounter within this profit driven society is that there is something terribly wrong with normal emotional response and healthy biological functioning. To be socially acceptable and correct we need to apply the notion of altering normal processes with chemicals, sometimes to an extent that fosters dissociation from the body. This is the climate in which substance abuse takes place- the commercial climate that profitably and legally encourages dependence on commercially marketed substances.

At the same time, public media delivers messages about the terrible consequences of illicit drug use. The "just say no" slogan of the "war on drugs" in the United States isn't specific enough or strong enough to counter pharmaceutical marketing campaigns and peer approved perks.

Children grow up watching parents use many commercially sanctioned chemical substances on and in their bodies. This becomes incorporated into a child's foundation learning about how the world functions, how normal adults function. The average person in the United States watches a minimum of 3 hours of television per day (Gentile & Walsh, 2002). Television is saturated with sophisticated pharmaceutical commercials depicting how delightful life can be after using a particular product.

Of course pharmaceuticals have a useful place in the world and I am very thankful for the remedial purpose many drugs serve. The simple reality, however, is that adults and children receive mixed messages about drug and alcohol use. Take drugs, lots of them, if they are prescribed by a doctor or purchased over the counter. Don't take the other drugs, even if they make you feel like the people on the television commercials appear to feel. Ask your doctor for that wonderful medication, even if you don't really need it, because it will likely make your life better. This is the climate in which we conduct drug and alcohol treatment.

Taking prescription or over the counter drugs as needed to remedy undesirable conditions is a socially sanctioned, common behavior in the United States and many modern countries. Indulging occasionally in recreational drugs or alcohol represents a common experience for many adults. Why then would anyone allow himself or herself to become dependent on or addicted to a chemical substance? Why would anyone establish a relationship with a substance capable of interfering with their optimal functioning? Why would anyone establish a relationship with a substance capable of doing serious damage to his or her body? Why would anyone develop a powerful intimate relationship with a substance to the exclusion of human intimacy? Why would anyone behaviorally prioritize a chemical substance over and above everything else?

Causes?

Many theories, from psychodynamic to physiological, attempt to explain how people develop dependent relationships with various substances. Literature on addictive tendencies, patterns, mechanisms and personality styles abounds. There may be much theoretical overlap between alcohol and other substances concerning causal factors of dependence. Understanding or even hypothesizing about specific contributors to addiction continues to inspire innovations in various forms of treatment. The disease model of alcoholism (Jellineck, 1960) functions as the backbone for twelve step recovery programs around the world. Menninger (1938) saw alcohol use as an individual's attempt to avoid a greater self-destruction related to childhood issues. Adler (1941) and McClelland (1972) place prime importance on the alcoholic's perception of personal power and enhanced esteem when drinking. Lisansky (1960) and McCord (1960) identify dependency needs and a dependence/independence conflict as central to their causal theory of alcoholism. Bateson (1972) suggested the particulars of communication play a role in the etiology of alcoholism (1986).

Biochemical research is exploring endogenous opioid feedback mechanisms possibly responsible for reinforcing alcohol consumption (O'Malley, 1995; DiChiara & Tanda, 1996; Gianoulakis, DeWaele & Thavundayil, 1996). These naturally occurring opioids, known as endorphins, play a role in stress response, immune function, reproductive biology, gastrointestinal function, cardiovascular status, mood change and response to pain (Kreek, 1998). Alteration of these same endogenous mechanisms is involved in heroin addiction (Kreek, 1998, Pert & Snyder, 1973). Research demonstrates how interference with the normal transport of the neurotransmitter dopamine plays a significant role in the misuse of cocaine and related drugs (Madras, 1999; Graybiel, 1999; Spitz & Rosecam, 1987). Manipulation of dopamine transport has also been linked to the maintenance of alcoholism (Markianos, Moussas, Lykouras & Hatzimanolis, 2000; Kreek, 1998). Pawlak (2001) speaks to the role of another neurotransmitter, serotonin, as she contends "there is biochemical proof of a serotonin dysfunction in most addictive problems."

Other studies have investigated the link between stress and alcoholism (Brown, Irwin & Schuckit, 1991; Grunberg & Klien, 1998), anxiety and alcoholism (Schuckit, Irwin & Brown, 1990) and stress and drug use (O'Doherty 1991; Shaham, 1993; Grunberg & Klein 1998; Weiss, 1999).

The roles that endorphins, dopamine, serotonin, norepinephrine, and GABA (gamma amino butyric acid) play in the biochemical theater of substance abuse are significant and well noted (Campbell, Kohl & McBride, 1996; Colvin, 1995; Foreman & Johansen, 1996; Galizio & Maisto, 1985; Graybiel, 1999; Inaba, Cohes & Holstein, 1997; Kreek, 1998; Madras, 1999; Markianos et al, 2000; Snyder, 1986; Unterwald, Horne-King & Kreek, 1992). These dynamic roles will be examined for relevance to *Utilization Sobriety* in Chapter Four. While we continue to learn more about the biochemical, behavioral and psychosocial dynamics of addiction, no evidence exists for a single cause of alcoholism or other addictive disorders. There are numerous factors contributing to this problem that demonstrate its complexity.

Treatment?

Treatment approaches, whether in outpatient or inpatient settings, encompass cognitive-behavioral therapy, pharmaceutical intervention, solution-focused therapy, harm reduction therapy, hypnosis, power interventions, incarceration, group therapy, support groups and more. Twelve step programs provide a dogma and structure composing the framework of myriad support groups vital to the sobriety of many. Many drug and alcohol treatment centers employ 12 step methods.

Alternatives for those not benefiting from or not compatible with the traditional AA (Alcoholics Anonymous) and NA (Narcotics Anonymous) twelve step orientation include treatment and support group approaches known as Rational Recovery (Trimpey, 1996) and Smart Recovery. These alternatives spring from the work of Albert Ellis (1988, 1971), one of the founding fathers of cognitive therapy. Women for Sobriety (WFS) is another alternative which emphasizes the power of positive emotions. An additional group, Secular Organization for Sobriety (SOS), has no spiritual foundation and maintains a goal of sobriety, one day at a time (Inaba & Cohen, 2004).

Neural stem cells normally divide throughout life and give rise to new neurons, a process known as neurogenesis. Research relevant to all forms of treatment indicates that chronic exposure to high and even moderate doses of alcohol interferes with the development of new neurons involved with hippocampal structure and function in the brain (Crews & Nixon, 2003, Nixon, 2006). The hippocampus plays a significant role in learning and memory. The good news for the person in recovery is that studies indicate after seven days abstinence from alcohol there begins a pronounced increase in new hippocampal neuron formation in animal models (Nixon & Crews, 2004).

Effective treatment for the offspring of substance using mothers demands significant consideration as a growing body of evidence demonstrates how fetal exposure to alcohol reduces serotonin innervation and compromises development of the forebrain along the serotonergic pathway (Zhou, Sari & Powrozek, 2005). Even moderate fetal alcohol exposure results in long-term, persistent defect in neurogenic responses to behavioral challenge (Choi, Allan &Cunningham, 2005). A growing body of research reflecting alcohol's detrimental influence on neurogenesis in fetal and adult development (Crews & Nixon, 2003, Nixon, 2005) supports behavioral training that promotes experience-dependent neuroplasticity or, in other words, the formation and change of brain neurons resulting from a specific experience. This treatment approach has been effective in a rat model of cerebellar damage induced by alcohol exposure during the period of brain development that is comparable to that of the human third trimester (Goodlett, Horn & Zhou, 2005). This treatment model is a conceptualization yet to be fully developed and applied to human treatment.

The literature both supports and challenges the efficacy of hypnotic approaches to substance abuse treatment. Some pose hypnotic methods for substance abuse treatment as uneventful, poorly defined or ill advised because of a lack of conclusive evidence to justify its application (Nash, 2001; Wadden & Penrod, 1981; Edwards, 1966). Stoil (1989) notes the many confounding factors involved in accurately evaluating the usefulness of hypnosis in treating alcoholism and the difficulty distinguishing hypnosis from the therapies to which it is applied. Successful outcomes cite the use of hypnosis as the sole treatment (Page & Handley, 1993) and hypnosis used in conjunction with other treatment methods (Orman, 1991; Vandamme, 1986).

Significant breakthroughs have been and are being made on the pharmaceutical front to curb drug and alcohol use. Among the many primary and supplementary drugs used, benzodiazepines and antabuse (disulfiram) have most commonly addressed alcohol withdrawal and sobriety maintenance. Naltrexone, an opiate antagonist, is now also being applied to sustain alcohol and cocaine abstinence. Variations of the synthetic opioid receptor ligand known as buprenorphine may soon be outpacing methadone for opiate withdrawal and maintenance. Many other drugs have been and are employed to support sobriety.

Research is piecing together some hopeful components of future alcohol treatment. With numerous remedial constructs, a growing body of empirical and scientific evidence and ongoing scientific advances, there remains no particular treatment formula that works for everyone. A treatment guide published by the National Institute on Drug Abuse (NIDA, 2000) simply states "No single treatment is appropriate for all individuals. Matching treatment strategies, interventions and services to each individual's particular problems and needs is critical to his or her ultimate success in returning to productive functioning in the family, workplace and society". Thus finding the right match of treatment to person and situation is an ongoing challenge.

Fortunately, we are gaining much clarity about the neurological and biochemical mechanisms of addiction. We have explanations for how particular substances lock into cellular receptor sites to alter the biochemical environment in the brain and elsewhere in the body. We have scientific explanations of how physiological dependence and addiction take form. The cellular and molecular communication involved in this process is fascinating and will be examined in more detail in Chapter Four. This understanding paved the way for the development of pharmacological interventions specific to particular substances of misuse. This is great news. So why hasn't substance abuse declined?

The user of a substance is getting something from the substance-state that is either needed, strongly desired or both. The substance-state refers primarily to the biochemical climate established in a human body after absorbing a particular substance. The secondary features of a substance-state include whatever alterations in perception, behavior, mood, cognition or processing dynamics that may coincide with the biochemical climate created by a substance. Investigation of both primary and secondary features of the substance-state ultimately gave birth to the notion of state-dependent learning (Overton, 1971, 1972) and, later, state-dependent memory, learning and behavior. The biochemical basis for state-dependent memory, learning and behavior is rooted in the information exchange between coded molecules collectively known as information substances and neuronal receptor sites (Pert, 1997, Rossi & Cheek, 1988).

Changing molecular chemistry to achieve sobriety eliminates only one part of the substance-state. The needs and desires the substance use addresses are still lingering and may even be screaming for amelioration. The social, environmental or circumstantial reinforcing cues of substance use may remain functionally in place. How a person responds to those cues or triggers depends much upon the particular nature of relationship that person has with the trigger related substance.

Level of severity

Healthcare professionals as well as the general public commonly draw distinctions between substance addiction, substance abuse, dependence on a substance and recreational use of a substance. Addiction encompasses dependence and is a compulsive, repetitive use of a substance in spite of terrible consequences such as illness, job loss, social limitations, blackouts and more. Psychobiological dependence on a substance invites withdrawal symptoms when the substance is no longer taken. Dependence may also be unrelated to addiction when a substance is employed for functional utility, as exemplified by trazodone or ambien for the insomniac.

All addictions, I believe, incorporate a biochemical

feedback mechanism providing organic incentive and motivation for repeated specific behaviors at a neuro-physiological level. I believe this is true of both addictions to chemical substances and endogenous addictive behaviors, known as process addictions, like gambling, spending, pornography and more. Some phase of an addictive behavior produces a felt sense of relief, excitement, satisfaction or completion needed by the addicted individual. With endogenous addictive behaviors, the sought after reward has a biochemical component. Endorphins, enkephalins, neurotransmitters and various peptides can all be part of the addictive state behavior and reward system.

Substance abuse, often coincidental with recreational use, is typically characterized by episodic, periodic or even single episode overindulgence in substance use. Serious consequences may or may not accompany the substance abuse. Ongoing repetitive dependent behavior common to addiction need not be present.

For our purposes and use of the *Utilization Sobriety* method, there is little need to distinguish between substance addiction, dependence, recreational use or abuse. A more practical approach considers a continuum of dependence on, and involvement with, a substance. The amount and frequency of substance use, tolerance and withdrawal dynamics, ability/inability to abstain, and the measure of physical, personal and social damage determine the degree of dependence for any individual. All of these factors reflect a person's position on a parallel continuum ranging from nonproblematic to extremely problematic. Physical and psychological dependence can occur simultaneously or independent of each other.

Applying a continuum which indicates a level of dependence and problematic effect fits well with a *harm reduction* model to treatment (Denning, 2000) and avoids the formation of pathological perspective.

Some substances not officially considered addictive are problematic for many people. Cannabis, or marijuana, falls into this category. If an individual wants to discontinue episodic use of a substance like cannabis or break an addictive pattern with any other substance, the initial phase of *Utilization Sobriety* treatment is the same. Follow up after establishing sobriety will conform to some basic principles applied in an individually tailored fashion.

•

We have examined some of the socio-cultural dynamics coloring drug use in general and substance abuse treatment in particular. A brief historical overview of perspectives of causal factors related to substance abuse ranged from psychodynamic to biochemical. Definition of the substance-state, with primary and secondary characteristics, implies a need to address much more than abstinence from a substance in treatment. For purposes of simplifying and unifying the *Utilization Sobriety* treatment, a substance use continuum is proposed.

Chapter Two

The Evolution of Utilization Sobriety

Each person is an individual. Hence, psychotherapy should be formulated to meet the uniqueness of the individual's needs, rather than tailoring the person to fit the Procrustean bed of a hypothetical theory of human behavior.
                    Milton H. Erickson

What if I said you really can experience the best aspects of using…?

<u>For instance</u>: Sam met with me a week after spending three months in jail. Having begun drinking alcohol and smoking marijuana as a teenager, Sam had a long history of consistent alcohol involvement, bar fights and outlaw associations. This forty-five year old, married, small business owner realized most of the problem spots in his life were associated with alcohol. Sam had been abstinent from alcohol for three months and sought help to maintain his sobriety. The last marijuana use by this client was reported to be five months prior to our first meeting. Sam defined marijuana smoking as his "anger management program."

I gathered much information from Sam about his substance use, the perceived benefits of alcohol use and his personal history. No prior mental health or substance abuse treatment was reported. Additional motivation for sobriety came from Sam's probation officer who demanded frequent drug testing.

I provided Sam with information about unconscious process and communication and elaborated on learning already stored in his system. I then asked him if he would like to employ his learning to support sobriety. He quickly affirmed this. I explained how Sam's unconscious mind has access to the desired information and how Sam could develop a signaling system with the unconscious by using his fingers. Sam was readily responsive to developing a yes and no signaling system with the unconscious. Without conscious intent, one finger lifted as a "yes" signal and another finger lifted as a "no" signal from Sam's unconscious mind.

I asked Sam "would it be alright to call up the very best aspects of drinking alcohol at this time…calling up the confidence, freedom from that self-consciousness and self-criticism… not taking things so personally, a good, warm feeling inside…?" (All benefits Sam had previously reported). Sam's "yes" finger lifted. A few minutes later, he spoke of the warm feeling in his throat and stomach, "just like after having a shot"(of whiskey), and a "clear comfort" with himself, and "a smooth rush." Sam developed a physical trigger to call up the best of the alcohol experience and was instructed to express his intention internally as he triggered the desired state.

Sam extended treatment another six sessions to address past trauma, unresolved emotional experience and his current circumstances. Significant progress was made and Sam adapted the alcohol tool he developed in treatment to all stressful situations successfully. He has remained free of any need to drink or smoke marijuana for one year. (Example previously cited in Walsh, 2003).

•

This book is basically a *how to* manual intended for any qualified healthcare provider working with people wanting to change their substance use habits. This is a manual describing how to help a person achieve sobriety quickly, safely and naturally. I attempt to get right to the essential pieces of what will be applicable and useful in your work with substance users. The type of substance being used by a person does not matter. The duration of use with some substances can, of course, affect cognitive functions and the way a person processes information provided to them. Cognitive limitations, in some cases, will require innovative adaptations of the approach presented here.

Utilization Sobriety has applied well in my practice to both the person wanting and needing absolute abstinence and the person desiring a reduction in substance usage. As a way of illustrating how I work with people and how I apply *Utilization Sobriety*, I will present a good portion of this book in a conversational manner similar to the exchange I would have with a client.

The method described here is simple, almost to

the point of embarrassment. Based on logic and observation, *Utilization Sobriety* requires nothing more than what the client brings into the office. I developed this approach out of frustration, among other things. I experienced much distress working in more conventional ways with substance abuse issues. It pained me to witness repeated relapse and people "white knuckling" their way through sobriety. Some people traded one addiction for another. Valid needs were frequently unmet by those struggling to maintain sobriety.

Relapse seems to be a part of any recovery process. I often share the story with clients of a man walking down a street, enjoying a beautiful day, and suddenly falling into a manhole missing its cover. The man climbed out of the manhole and said he would never make that mistake again. The next day he walked down the same street and only saw the open manhole at the last minute. His momentum couldn't overcome his awareness and he plunged into the hole. The third day he walked down the same street and walked around the manhole. The fourth day he walked down a different street. We learn from mistakes and can eventually get it right.

Of course there is a lot more to a person than an addiction and often too little treatment time available to address other salient issues. In spite of all the practical, limiting realities inherent in providing drug and alcohol treatment, I desperately wanted to find a different way of doing this work.

While working in a community mental health agency, a rich variety of clients from widely disparate income levels helped me explore various treatment options in a fail-safe manner. Narrative therapy (White, 1990, 1993) helped some reconstruct their life perspective enough to inspire change. Cognitive approaches, more attune to Albert Ellis's Rational Emotive Therapy (Ellis, 1971, Ellis et al, 1988), helped some challenge entrenched thought patterns and examine consequences enough to commit to change. Solution focused approaches found merit with some by expanding perspective and affirming self-regulation (deShazer, 1988, Miller & Berg 1995). Formal hypnosis yielded some good short term results for some by recruiting inner resources needed to achieve sobriety. I found premature psychodynamic exploration often gave people reason to consume more substance.

All the approaches I applied had some benefit for some people and little perceived benefit for others. No single approach, of the many being applied to drug and alcohol treatment, is always successful. Success, as applied here, refers to sobriety and does not account for other subjective benefits a client may derive. As scientific inquiry into the etiology and psychosocial parameters of substance addictions continues, it is clear that individuals idiosyncratically respond to a perceived need by using a substance of choice.

After examining my clinical experience against the history of drug and alcohol treatment up to the present and looking at various theoretical explanations for dependence on substance, I synthesized the following hypothesis.

Consider the likelihood that **IF** a person can move from an external locus of dependence to an internal position of control and self-reliance (Blane, 1968; Knight, 1937; Menninger, 1938; McCord & McCord, 1960), and if a person likewise moves from a sense of helplessness toward autonomy and an awareness of personal power (McClelland, 1972), and if treatment is integrative and considers the whole person (Jung, 1933; Maslow, 1970), and if psychobiological needs are acknowledged and respected, and if the client's own system and process is utilized (Erickson, Rossi & Rossi 1976), and a new cognitive framework is added which bypasses shame and perceived resistance, **THEN** substance use will not be emotionally driven or part of a cognitive/perceptual network sustaining prior beliefs and learning about self and the world. Substance use thus becomes a redundant, maladaptive choice, no longer a need or mechanism for satisfying a need.

So how does one accommodate for all these qualifiers? Where are the pieces to this puzzle? The answers came from a number of sources. The first involves my personal experience and clinical work with clients that informed me well about the benefits of *screening for client strengths* and *tapping into unconscious resources*. Holding a perspective conducive to recognizing and employing client strengths will be more fully explained in the next chapter.

Unconscious Communication

Tapping into the unconscious resources and communicating directly with the unconscious is what hypnosis is all about. Formal hypnosis is but one avenue to pursue the unconscious. Active imagination (Stein, 1985), a dream interpretation approach developed by Carl Young, involves direct communication with the unconscious employing dream imagery. The empty chair technique of Gestalt Therapy (Perls, 1979) is an effective tool reliant upon trance phenomena experienced by a client as hallucination, time distortion or age regression. Effective Gestalt work very much engages unconscious process. Transactional Analysis (Berne, 1964) is another therapeutic treatment dependent on unconscious communication and process. The Holotropic Breathwork developed by Stanislov Groff (1985) clearly aims to access the unconscious. Applied Kinesiology (Frost, 2002), a practice popular with chiropractors and other alternative medicine practitioners, relies on unconscious communication or ideomotor expression (i.e. body language).

An approach I find particularly useful for communicating with the unconscious is called *ideomotor questioning*. The term "ideomotor" is based on the Latin root *ideo*, meaning idea and *motor*, meaning movement. "Yes" and "no" signals from the unconscious are established through finger movement. One finger lifting up or moving is a "yes" signal and a different finger lifting up is a "no" signal. Ideomotor communication was employed by Milton Erickson (1976) and systematically applied and defined by Cheek and LeCron (1968). Rossi

(1986) and Cheek (1988) beautifully elaborate on more than finger signals as they illustrate applications of this form of unconscious expression. Ideomotor questioning is incorporated in the *Utilization Sobriety* method and requires no hypnotic induction. Ideomotor signals are really just a narrow variation on body language. Any presentation of affect, physical posturing or gesturing can embody conscious intention and unconscious expression singularly, in harmonic communion with each other or expressively opposed and conflicted. Is not body language the primary domain and native dialect of the unconscious?

State-Dependent Learning, Memory and Behavior

A second piece of the puzzle resulted from the generous contributions of Donald Overton. Overton (1971, 1972, 1973 & 1982) accumulated evidence and conducted experiments to verify the psychobiological phenomenon of state-dependent learning. State-dependent learning is about information being channeled through or contained in a particular physiological state. The concept has now been expanded to state-dependent memory, learning and behavior. Evidence supporting how specific learning can be contained in states of intoxication or arousal made me wonder about accessing memory of the state itself. If a particular physiological state holds specific memories, learning and behavior, what benefits might be derived from accessing a physiological memory of the state? This is where the unconscious comes into play.

Some approaches to psychotherapeutic treatment are

successful because, I believe, the approach accesses and modifies specific state-dependent memory, learning or behavior somehow involved with undesirable symptoms. Consider the following examples.

At a presentation I attended, Aaron Beck, a founding father of cognitive therapy, demonstrated an innovative approach to help people manage panic and anxiety. Beck provided information about physical response to hyperventilation and guided his volunteer subject through a modified hyperventilation exercise. The subject was instructed to signal when ready to stop the exercise. The implication is that the subject is in charge and able to stop the process. Beck joined the subject and modeled accelerated breathing. The symptoms resulting from hyperventilation are very similar to symptoms of panic- tingling in extremities and face, flush, sweaty palms, increased pulse, some vertigo, etc. As symptoms develop and the subject signals readiness to end the exercise, the subject is instructed to exhale deeply and completely, inhale slowly and deeply, developing a more natural exchange of air. The pseudo-panic attack is contained and managed effectively.

What really happens with this elegant approach to managing panic? Communication from the therapist is delivered and likely received on a number of different levels. A client, for example, may be getting any of the following messages:

"You are going to create some symptoms and eliminate those symptoms just for the heck of it. The symptoms are physical manifestations of something under your control. You are in charge of the symptoms. You can have these symptoms without any fearful thoughts and without anything horrible happening. You can change your breathing pattern to manage any real panic."

Another dynamic taking place elicits components of the physiological state related to panic and anxiety. Hyperventilation modifies the biochemical environment in the body. As blood oxygen levels change, the hypothalamus sends signals to activate the adrenals and more. At the very least, significant portions of the state involved in panic are accessed and embellished. The state is summoned in a safe, controlled environment. The element of conscious control and regulation is added to a state previously seen as out of control. Information possibly contained in this state can be accessed incidentally without trying to search it out. Very useful information has surfaced in my work with people using this approach.

Another approach popularized by Stanislov Groff, M.D. (1985) is called Holotropic Breathing. This also incorporates hyperventilation. The subject is encouraged to be receptive to whatever develops as the pace of breathing is increased. The subject is reminded about remaining absolutely safe in spite of what material may surface or how the subject may express the experience.

Again, with Holotropic Breathwork, the state reminiscent of anxiety, panic or profound stress is accessed along with whatever memory, learning, emotion or behavior that state might contain.

The substance using state is the sum total of the physiological and perceptual experience. The term "state" refers primarily to a particular physiological, biochemical reality. That organic matrix almost always affects emotion, perception, thought and often behavior, singularly or collectively. The term "state" reveals itself as observable affect. This propensity demands a broader definition of state. For example, when I refer to someone in a very inebriated state, more than just a particular blood alcohol level comes to mind. Inebriation cradles a set of characteristics and potentials involving perceptual distortion, cognitive distortion, behavioral alteration, mood lability and more.

So the term state, as used in this text, implies more than just a physiological position. The affective experience (incorporating emotion, emotional expression, responsive idiosyncrasies and body language) accompanying a state change certainly speaks to the integration and indivisibility of mind and body. Thinking in terms of state dependent learning, memory and behavior provided me with a useful framework from which to explore various possibilities.

Tapping into a substance-state holds great potential for accessing useful information bound by that state.

The Utilization Principle

A third part of the puzzle came from Milton Erickson (1976, 1979). A major contribution Erickson made to the field of psychotherapy is the *utilization principle*. This construct reflected the way Erickson worked. It illuminates the functional utility of incorporating what a client brings to therapy into the therapeutic process. Client experience and learning, current circumstances and peculiarities, client words and client ways of being all represent raw material from which to construct therapeutic interventions. This same raw material serves to color the treatment provider's orientation to present and future possibilities for the client.

Erickson explained "By using the patient's own patterns of response and behavior, including those of their actual illness, one may effect therapy more promptly and satisfactorily, with resistance to therapy greatly obviated and acceptance of therapy facilitated." (in Rossi, 1980, Vol. 4)

Upon first examination, Erickson's work had enormous appeal to my senses of logic and creativity. Treatment is geared to the unique qualities and characteristics of the client. Sometimes Erickson helped a person resolve a problem by prescribing a problematic symptom in a specific manner, as the following example illustrates.

For the religious woman who withdrew socially after loudly passing gas in a classroom, Erickson spoke to God's superb design of a valve that opened downward and held in liquids and solids while letting only gas through. He instructed her to go have a big pot of beans and practice making big ones, little ones, loud one and soft ones The woman followed through with Erickson's instructions and ultimately returned to the classroom (Rosen, 1982).

Sometimes Erickson employed what the client perceived as physical flaws to build ego strength and beneficially alter client self-perception. This seemed to me a very practical, non-pathologizing way to work with people.

The *utilization principle* birthed in me a *strengths perspective*. It caused me to ask what parts of client reality can possibly be woven into treatment or used as treatment.

Physiological Basis of Body-mind Communication

Another piece of the puzzle was derived from scientific evidence defining the complexities of body-mind communication and lending more credence to the deep levels of state-dependent memory, learning and behavior. The efforts of Candice Pert (1973. 1985, 1997) are greatly appreciated in this regard. Her ground breaking work with neuropeptides and receptor sites yielded scientific evidence for how so much body-mind communication takes place.

Principles of Body-mind Healing

Ernest Rossi's work helped enormously to weave a number of puzzle pieces together. His integration of empirical realities, scientific substance and the utilization principle fueled daring formulation of theories and constructs explaining the principles of body-mind communication and healing (1986, 1993). Rossi's postulates and practical therapeutic application of evidence continue to inspire me.

Connecting the pieces

Assembling the puzzle pieces described above allows me to present a commonsense way to work with people to change their substance use habits. By acknowledging, respecting and utilizing the gestalt a person brings to treatment, the process is kept simple and quite individualized. Treatment can then be responsive to myriad possible causal factors. This approach attempts to:

- idiosyncratically utilize the client psychobiological system

- affirm and empower clients to enhance self-esteem

- incorporate a mechanism for relapse prevention

- foster change without eliminating coping strategies employed by the client

- provide a safe foundation for addressing the client's mental health themes related to substance misuse, without segregating substance abuse from mental health.

The practitioner, whether a mental health or medical professional, need not have any prior training or expertise in areas of unconscious communication, unconscious process, hypnosis, ideomotor questioning or biochemistry. The elemental information necessary to learn and apply the *Utilization Sobriety* procedure is included in this text.

●

Hopefully this chapter has provided you with some sense of how the pieces of *Utilization Sobriety* came together. A strengths perspective applied to clinical work was referenced and will soon be elaborated upon. Working directly with the unconscious to access resources in that realm was an important piece. The contributions I absorbed from Donald Overton about state-dependent learning, from Milton Erickson about utilization and unconscious communication, from Candice Pert about physiological communication, from Ernest Rossi and David Cheek about ideomotor questioning and from Ernest Rossi about sewing it all together have resulted in yet another approach to treating substance abuse.

Chapter Three

Source of Strength

Look well into thyself; there is a source of strength which will always spring up if thou wilt always look there.
Marcus Aurelius

What if I said you really can experience the best aspects of…?

<u>For instance</u>: Tom did not seek help initially for substance abuse. This twenty-five year-old, bright self-employed man desperately wanted relief from panic attacks. He reported panic attacks beginning six years earlier after he stopped a six-month exploration of "crystal meth" (methamphetamine). Many trips to the emergency room and his primary care physician found nothing wrong with his heart. Panic was tied to an obsessive focus on heart rhythm, as Tom vigilantly awaited a missed beat.

Tom said the attacks usually came in the evening or weekends when he wasn't at work. Alcohol, he discovered, offered him relief from panic and thoughts about his heart. He didn't want to continue drinking at the level he had acquired but needed to stop the panic attacks first. Aside from smoking cigarettes and drinking alcohol, Tom reported no other drug use over the past six years. He did share that he only gets the attacks if he is smoking cigarettes.

I asked Tom to tell me about all the positive elements related to his drinking. He identified specific features of the intoxication process from which he captured his greatest relief. I reflected how Tom has the learning about intoxication in him and how he can access that information through the unconscious mind. Tom developed a yes/no signaling system with the unconscious as a particular finger lifted up to signal "yes" or "no". Tom "dryly" called up that specific relief state and developed a way of retrieving the experience as desired.

Tom conquered the anxiety using his "alcohol tool" and excavated the trauma related to an experience he had all too quickly dismissed as nothing. Processing this reality afforded Tom a much more peaceful, forward motion perspective.

◆

I would be amiss to neglect some discussion about foundation principles inherent in all my clinical work. The following elaborates on a clinical orientation that scans for whatever client strengths, resources or potentials may be instrumental in achieving a clinical goal. This orientation also examines the structure supporting inner strengths involved in both healthy change and detrimental rigidity.

This chapter reflects an umbrella perspective from

which I work, regardless of the particular intervention I am applying or the particular theoretical orientation guiding that intervention. The perspective is essentially a *goal directed strengths perspective*. It provides a lens through which I attempt to see a unique individual who has somehow managed to navigate through life's mixed offerings up to the present moment. Through this lens I glimpse the environment and circumstances the client deals with day by day. Through this lens I attempt to recognize what has allowed this person to get to *now*. In what ways has a person experienced mastery (i.e. learning to swim, getting a driver's license) in the past? What resources and experience reflect strength, motivation and resourcefulness coming from within? What client attributes, attitudes and ways of being will help this treatment work successfully? What successes of the past might be revived, applied or amplified?

Bear with me as I elaborate on themes possibly quite familiar to you. I take this liberty for a number of reasons. The *goal directed strengths perspective* was the lens I looked through as the *Utilization Sobriety* procedure evolved. This lens allowed me to contemplate state-dependent learning as well as accessing unconscious resources to employ that learning. This lens inspires a belief that most of the time most people have within them the raw material needed to construct a solution to their problem. I stress "most" because sometimes a person is lacking something we mistakenly assume is there. This then begs for the addition of a few essential ingredients to the mix.

This elaboration also relates to the mechanics of establishing a responsive, functional treatment climate. Themes and information I share with clients in some fashion, often early in the treatment process, will be referenced. Some clients want and need a lot of information about how treatment works or how *anything* can possibly work with them. Some need to know more about how I perceive them in order to reinforce or rebuke shame. Particular types of information will be necessary to fuel motivation at times. Some will need only a few details before giving the go ahead for treatment.

Items contributing to this discussion on strengths include:

- The development of inner reality
- Personal history
- Humor
- Belief and Meaning
- Spiritual relatedness
- Choice
- Time orientation
- Sensory presence
- Language
- The problem

Inner Reality

Lets look at how individualized reality in the human system gets started. From the beginning, inner reality is forming and expanding with added experience. An instinctually preserving and protecting intelligence within uses whatever it has to assure psychobiological survival and wellness. Information and experience fund learning, perception and belief. What any person holds to be real is a result of that person's perceptions and beliefs.

Consensus reality is a collective grouping of similar perceptions and beliefs demonstrating mass agreement about what is real and true. At one time in history consensus reality declared the world to be flat. Objective scientific measurement, most often dependent on the technology of the day, offers some certainty about external reality and a persuasive influence on the inner reality of the mind.

Each individual, I believe, comes into the world with purity, potential, value and worth. From the very beginning an infant is rapidly absorbing information, learning what the world is about, learning functions and limitations, learning how the world relates to him or her. The entire growing up process, moving from infancy to adulthood, is about building an *inner foundation of reality*. That inner reality foundation is composed of many experiential bricks. Each new experience demands a place in the foundation. What does the experience mean? What does the experience say about how the world works? What does the experience say about how I fit in the world? What kind of emotional response do I have to that experience? What kind of emotional response do others have to this experience? Somehow that initial experience becomes a new piece of foundation reality which functions as a reference point.

Reference points and their associated networks are lodged neurologically in different parts of the brain and body. Among the complex web of neural pathways, the hippocampus and amygdala together record and assign emotion to experience. Memory destined to be long-term is eventually embedded in the cortex. Molecular information substances circulate information between various organ systems and the central nervous system.

Because inner reality is constructed from an individual's unique experience and learning, no two people have the same inner reality. My inner reality is the unique experience of me, a composite of all that has come before in my life; all learning and experience, dreams and disappointments, successes and failures, skills and abilities, potentials not yet realized. Inner reality involves the sum total of an individual interacting with current circumstances, current choices and possibilities, and current emotional response to the perception of now. Your perception of now is your current inner reality. How you see, hear, feel, touch, taste, smell and think about the world is a big chunk of inner reality. How you see and experience yourself in the world and in relationship to others is another big piece of your inner reality.

Whether a person's current reality is desirable or undesirable, it is essentially a judgment free orientation resulting from the accumulation of all that has come before. A person's behavior, however, is quite subject to judgment. Inner reality is cumulative and always subject to change, in spite of feeling intractable at times. Experience has demonstrated that change is always happening. Our inner reality is always accumulating new experience and learning. Circumstances change and we have choices about how we deal with those circumstances.

Two people may have a similar experience, but how they respond to it and how they absorb or shield the experience is unique to them. There is no right or wrong about anyone's inner reality. It is just a result of life experience, particularly during the growing up years. We make judgments about what we do and the actions that affect others.

A judgment-free inner reality runs counter to the dogma of many religions. Growing up Catholic, I was taught that my thoughts could earn me real estate in Hell. I always had some reason to feel guilty. This was my early practical training for cognitive therapy, as there was great incentive to practice thought stopping and cognitive restructuring. A judgment-free inner reality was not part of my early foundation.

Each piece of foundation reality may be summed up in a simple sentence or two like: "I am a creative person", or "I am a slow learner", or "Hard work pays off" or " I am pretty/ugly" or "I will never really succeed" or "I am smart." A web of behaviors, perceptions, emotions, beliefs and more, however, surrounds that piece of reality. Over time we connect more and more experience to the foundation. This reinforces our inner reality as the inner reality guides perception of the world and ourselves. The process is cyclic and self-perpetuating.

At least some portion of inner reality is constructed solely to help us survive the growing up years at a psychological and emotional level. As we move through adulthood, some pieces of our inner reality may not fit the reality of who we are and may even be counterproductive to our best interest and intention. We are then challenged to rework pieces of inner reality.

Inner reality poses as a perceptual and referential guide for maneuvering through the world. It is one part of an extensive non-conscious intelligence within each individual. That non-conscious intelligence which embodies the unconscious mind can be considered an expert consultant on self. It has been there since the beginning. It knows all about past experience and the learning and emotion tied to experience. It knows all about the unique characteristics and qualities that make someone who they are. It knows about the skills, abilities and potentials within. It is tapped into the biological functions of the body and can sometimes have a significant influence on those functions. The unconscious mind has a wonderful production crew that puts on a show during sleep time. There is so much creative energy in the dream world and it all comes from within. So many useful resources lie within the grasp of the unconscious.

The unconscious mind is there to help. It works for us 24 hours of every day. It has your basic survival needs foremost in mind. Biological functions like blood pressure, pulse, vascular dilation, body temperature, kidney function, gastrointestinal functions and all the operations of the autonomic nervous system are influenced by unconscious process for your welfare.

Emotional and physical symptoms often develop as signals from the unconscious that something needs to change. Fears and phobias may develop as a way of protecting a person from perceived physical or emotional harm. Post-traumatic stress disorder is an extreme and complicated example of that protective function.

Inner reality is timeless, as is the protective function of that expert consultant. Even critical messages coming from within likely had a purposeful, protective function in the beginning. As we mature to adulthood, we have many more choices with accumulated experience and learning. We understand ourselves a bit more. Those limiting, critical messages may be anachronisms, completely incompatible with who we really are and the real potentials that lie within us. This is when the important energy involved in protective functions needs to be updated and redirected in helpful ways.

The unconscious is always communicating at some level. The body is a wonderful vehicle of expression for the unconscious. Contained emotions are often expressed through the body as some variation of gastrointestinal distress or a pain in the neck or a skin irritation or spontaneous lacrimation (tearing). Pleasant emotions come through as laughter, tears of joy, a warm flush or a sigh of relief. Body language, of course, says much.

A network of molecular information substances is always transmitting information between the central nervous system and various organ systems throughout the body. This communication involves emotional status and immune function. The unconscious mind receives information from all the sensory channels to register taste, smell, touch, sound and sight as a component of whatever experience is taking place.

Information coming from the external world affects communication internally in order to orchestrate an appropriate response. For instance, hearing a fire alarm may prompt activation of the hypothalamic fight/flight/freeze response and a rapid change of physiological state. Internally generated information, void of any real external threat, can also inspire the same response under the guise of anxiety and panic. The person experiencing panic attacks has evidence reflecting a well functioning, albeit over functioning, emergency response system.

Inner reality embodies foundation beliefs and learning potentially at the root of both abundant resources and confounding limitations. Inner reality is malleable and changing as new information linked to new experience and learning is added and dysfunctional pieces of foundation are ideally reconstructed. An inviting curiosity held by the treatment provider about how a client's inner reality will navigate through treatment serves to bypass judgment and shame induction.

Personal history

The dynamic exchange at the intersection of external events and inner reality says much about our personal history. In addition to contributing to the foundation of inner reality, personal history provides a wonderful lens through which to view many strengths. The accomplishments, successes, important learning, ability to learn, joyful experiences, adaptive innovations, means of accumulating useful skills and much more are all part of a lifelong history. Too often this is taken for granted, discounted entirely or minimized. When one is reminded of the tremendous challenge met as a child to learn to ride a bike, walk, tie a shoe or swim, inner resources are often automatically summoned or acknowledged. Past experience says a lot about a person's coping skills, survival strategies and resourcefulness. Everyone has had to traverse difficult situations. Everyone has experienced loss, even though they may not recognize it as such until it is brought to their attention. Everyone has accomplished something. The fact that a person made it to your office is a commendable accomplishment.

Humor

How a person accesses or employs humor speaks to a significant area of resourcefulness. Certainly humor can be seen as an avoidance strategy. It can also be seen as a coping strategy. It is often a social emulsifier or a way of providing momentary shelter from an emotional storm. Humor sometimes positions absurdity in a less personalized and more workable place. Humor is one way to escape the gravity of any situation that otherwise makes no sense or has no meaning. Laughing can create some insulation from circumstances and beneficially release accumulated affect.

Humor also establishes meaning and provides even momentary levity and reprieve from difficult situations. A brief reprieve can allow different parts of the self to reorganize or adjust to the environment in a way that reduces stress on one's internal system, facilitating health. The ability to access humor reflects strength.

Meaning

What meaning does your client attribute to his or her experience? Maybe none. Maybe there is a message intertwined with spiritual relatedness or a particular belief. Constructing or uncovering a novel reality that explains experience can positively alter otherwise restrictive emotional, intellectual and even physiological states. Frankl's existential theory (1959) and White's (1990, 1993) deconstruction treatment rest heavily on our ability to influence internal experience and external behavior by the meaning we ascribe to events.

Frankl believes that we are challenged to change ourselves when we are unable to change our situation. By changing our attitude toward our suffering we give meaning to it, and gain the will to fight to survive our suffering.

Belief

From our personal history of experience and learning we construct a reality. Beliefs and learning are the building blocks of a psychic foundation and link our personal reality to peerless perspective. Cognitive therapies

(Beck, 1976. Ellis, 1971) operate on the premise that beliefs can be altered to influence emotions, behaviors and thoughts. Powerful experience and human interactions can alter belief. The building blocks of any preconstructed reality or belief can be adjusted, rearranged, amplified or even disregarded in response to situational demands or scrutiny.

A seriously obese religious woman came to realize she binged food as a way of "punishing" herself for "mistakes" she made raising her children. Only after she imagined trading places with a compassionate God could she stop the binge pattern. Her belief in a compassionate God was employed therapeutically. This allowed her to see she had suffered enough to pay for her "wrongs." Existing beliefs can be employed to affect change.

Many (Simonton, Chopra, Cousins, Siegel, Rossi) have demonstrated how belief can alter physiological processes, reverse disease and even postpone death.

Human need for approval, recognition and acceptance often so powerfully guides belief and behavior that it almost seems instinctual. This natural and often covert quest for approval powerfully influences motivation, belief, and activity from infancy on through adulthood. Like a biological positive and negative feedback mechanism in which a demand automatically elicits the corresponding compensatory readjustment, so we respond to our social environment.

What client belief might serve to fuel motivation or reinforce new behaviors?

Spirit

The lens of spiritual relatedness acknowledges an unknown, something greater than the self to which we are somehow connected. The baseline belief of mystery provides a fluid context to which meaning can be ascribed or attributed. The transcendence of experience becomes possible, even when events shatter previously held beliefs and reality, because one is part of something greater than any belief or discomfort. Spirituality can be attached to helpful or harmful beliefs.

Many have reported a kind of spiritual awakening after losing and then finding a sense of self and purpose through a devastating experience. Spiritual meaning of ones connection to self, others and the universe is a private and powerful experience defying adequate definition for purposes of this text.

What spiritual beliefs or inclinations does this client hold which may strengthen the changes he or she desires?

Time

The nature of time has fascinated and has confounded humanity throughout history. While we can accurately measure the passage of time with atomic clocks, we know little about the biophysics of our ability to manipulate internal time (expand, condense) or reposition ourselves on the time-space axis (someplace in the past, present or future). We can scan various positions (i.e.. the environment we grew up in, a job we're trying to secure, etc.) on the time continuum and also experience those positions in some fashion. We can affix particular beliefs to various temporal bases.

Hopes and dreams are based on "time travel" into the future and belief anchored in the future. Anxiety almost always involves fear attached to something that has not yet happened in objective reality. While sleeping, a vivid dream covering a span of a year can occur during a few minutes of clock time. An old familiar song can instantly take us back to an experience many years ago. Real threat and physical pain commonly concentrate experience in the present, making it difficult to remember the past. This temporal malleability permits us to alter and create much of our experience.

What position on the time continuum will serve my client's best interest during this phase of treatment? What parts of treatment would best serve the client by associating with past experience of expanded time, when five minutes of clock time seems like an hour? Or condensed time when an hour of clock time seems like five minutes?

Sensory Presence

A powerful means of perceiving or experiencing inner strength is through the senses. Although any of the five senses are excellent vehicles for "time travel" (i.e. The smell of carnations taking us back in time to a funeral service), they also provide a remarkable medium by which to be fully present at an essential level. Essential, in this context, refers to the essence of self, the primal core with which inherent strength, resources, knowledge and instinct resonate.

Consider the continuum of time as a seesaw, such that *past* and *future* are at opposite ends of the plank and present rests just above the fulcrum on which the seesaw pivots. When the plank is heavily weighted by the *future*, an individual usually is experiencing either anxiety, preoccupation with achieving a goal or realizing change or fantasy. When the plank is heavily weighted by the *past*, one is usually experiencing depression, grief, a conditioned response or review. Experience of the present requires a level balance of the plank. Actively tuning into *present* sensory experience usually brings awareness into the *now*. The leveling process incorporates past learning and experience, creative personal expression, awareness of or plan for the *future*, confidence in survival and somatic dynamics.

As one begins to deeply explore any combination of sensory input in the present, acquired conscious congestion and activity is set aside without giving up conscious facility. What all am I hearing, seeing, tasting, smelling, feeling now? The insulation around the essential self, which may include persona, defenses, dogma and more, is penetrated. Uncovered is the essence containing both phylogenic and ontogenic potential present at birth. This includes evolving identity, full range of emotion and sensation, instinctual validity, creativity, adaptability, generativity, connectedness regarding universal process and significant strength and energy for survival.

Even staying fully present with suffering through the sensory channel can be an avenue to the resources of the core self. Suffering becomes something outside of the self, not the self. As others (Frankl, Gilligan, Jung, Erickson) have discussed, a consequence of being fully present is recognizing that one is more than just the suffering. The "stuff" extraneous to the self can and does change.

As my client learns how to be fully present through

sensory attunement, does she recognize her ability to shift temporal position and even navigate around anxiety? How might she extend the duration of the feeling related to the very pleasant memory? What upcoming activities might trigger that pleasant memory, as a useful resource?

Language

Looking through the lens of language permits much about strength and style to be identified. The use of tense (past, present, future) can both define and shift one's position on the time continuum. Pronouns may illustrate involvement or detachment. Prepositions (if, when, where, what, how, why) describe temporal position, certainty/uncertainty, confidence, probability, etc. Verbs are active or passive. Gregory Bateson (1971, 1972) researched the microdynamics of communication extensively to define the profound power and influence words have.

The language of psychotherapy has too often been weighted with pejorative, inflexible and hopeless terminology. Language can just as easily inspire hope, reflect integrity or self-perception, create confusion, distinguish self from other, reveal an orientation and much more.

The client's language commonly reflects how information is processed. Most people process information initially through visual, auditory or kinesthetic modalities. Other processing modalities such as taste and smell are less common. The particular modality being endorsed is typically manifest in language. For instance, if a client says "I *felt* vulnerable a few times at the interview as they *pummeled* me with questions," I assume the speaker has a kinesthetic orientation. Information is processed initially through the felt sense. The language of feeling, metaphoric or literal, links to experience and thought. Hearing "I *see* that you are *targeting* a promotion from the way you *flash* through that door every day" directs me to the speaker's application of a visual processor.

This understanding is employed extensively by people who teach or apply neurolinguistic programming (NLP) (Bandler & Grinder, 1979). The primary processing modality (known to NLP practitioners as the *representational system*) used by a client reflects an peculiar communication style. This well developed linguistic filter is a strength and can be employed as such.

What client words or manner of speaking reveal resources potentially useful for realizing treatment goals?

Choice

All living things respond to a dynamic momentum toward expression. Plants express buds, flowers, and scents. Insects express through color, behavior, colonization, sound and growth. Mothers express milk for newborns. While much expression in humans is beyond the scope of choice (i.e. cellular growth and specialization), much is left to choice. Socio-cultural norms and conditioning often imply no choice because of man's inherent craving for approval and dread of censure. We may forget about autonomy as a choice that may be contrary to particular group standards or cohesion. Even when environmental contingencies are severely limited, internal psychic constructs and perceptions remain under the influence of choice. Exercising choice can contribute to whatever degree of control is necessary for maintenance of psychological stability. This is an expression of self and reflects some aspect of personal identity.

Victor Frankl (1959) wrote extensively about choice. It was during Frankl's most extreme experience of deprivation and confinement in a Nazi concentration camp that he realized a level of choice few of us consider. Frankl had lost everything - all his worldly possessions, the people closest to him, his freedom. He was confined in crowded barracks with the sick and dying. There seemed to be no choice about anything. In the depths of great despair, Frankl realized he had choice about whether or not to talk to the people around him. He had choice about what to say if he chose to speak. He had choice about how he focused his thoughts. He could dwell on the misery around him, or on all he had lost, or on a pleasant experience of the past, or a fantasy of liberation. He had real choice about thinking. He had choice about whether he ate a ration of food or not. He could choose to die before other circumstances took his life. Frankl demonstrated that from the micro to the macro, we always have choices.

Recognizing and exercising choice in any fashion is a lens by which to see or express strength. It has been said that freedom means choosing your burden. Carrying a burden requires strength.

Consider choosing to give or receive a gift. For those who decide to accept a gift from another, there may be a realization of joy, a sense of being recognized, accepted or appreciated, a sense of connection, self-worth or something else. These conditions speak of the power and strength implicit in "gifting" another. A gift may be an approving look/gesture/word, a compliment, a promise, an exchange of goods or anything freely given. The giver may recognize a heightened sense of personal control, worth, or mastery as even a minimal feedback loop reinforces his/her gifting behavior. This behavior fosters reciprocity and is a vital component of community, being connected to something larger than self, belonging.

Does my client recognize he always has choices at some level? What choice is my client exercising at this time that is in his best interest?

The Problem

Examining all dimensions of almost any presenting problem reveals an assortment of strengths. The obvious problem example for this text is drug and alcohol abuse. *Utilization Sobriety* recognizes learning, even at a physiological level, about a substance and about the needs a substance serves. Drug or alcohol use may have begun as a coping strategy or a social emulsifier or a prescribed medical intervention. The person showing up for treatment likely has some level of courage and desire for change. Learning, coping strategies, courage and motivation all serve survival needs and reflect strength.

Consider the person with obsessive-compulsive features as another example. This person pays great attention to detail and has superb recall. Remarkable skill with organization and observation often accompany this disorder as well. Creativity about mapping the future, albeit typically skewed in a catastrophic manner that fuels anxiety, represents another resource commonly displayed in the obsessive-compulsive spectrum. Many more examples will likely come to you as you consider the full dimension of any problem situation or disorder.

◆

This is far from an exhaustive list of lenses through which to see clients. Each individual presents a different inner reality from which many useful strengths and resources can be derived. The source of limiting beliefs and behaviors may also be a part of inner reality's foundation, in need of upgrading. We have looked at how personal history can uncover personal assets. Humor is always a benefit. Meaning and belief often function as the backbone reinforcing desirable change. Spiritual context and relatedness provide needed support for many and access dimensions of faith and belief. One's orientation in time and perception of time have a very direct influence on how present experience is perceived. Tuning into the sensory experience of the present has great merit and reflects strength. Recognizing the choices available at different levels of experience augments personal power, autonomy and a sense of personal control sometimes needed to maintain psychological stability. The presenting concern or problem often holds the components of solution.

Adopting this strengths perspective allows any psychotherapeutic treatment to flow more smoothly. This orientation is built into the *Utilization Sobriety* procedure and is, I believe, a vital part of its effectiveness.

Chapter Four

Body-Mind Communication

Our remedies oft in ourselves do lie, which we ascribe to Heaven.
Shakespeare

What if I said you really can experience the best...?

<u>For instance</u>: Lou called my office in desperation and said he was obsessing about heroin and afraid he couldn't resist it without some help. He wanted to know if hypnosis might help. Lou was seen that afternoon. Lou was a 30 year-old self-employed craftsman and single parent. Lou had been smoking heroin for a number of months, convincing himself he could stop any time he chose. Lou had experienced many other drugs in the past. He said he had been clean for at least a week and realized he could easily "flush life down the drain" if he continued using. Lou had no history of substance abuse treatment.

Information was gathered about the best parts of the heroin experience and the needs it addressed. Lou was informed about unconscious communication and process. I referenced the physiological learning Lou already had about heroin and many other state-bound experiences. I asked Lou "if it were possible to experience the best qualities of the heroin use without the actual drug, would you be interested?" Lou said yes and then developed "yes" and "no" ideomotor finger signals. I asked the question, "Is it alright to call up the best aspects of a very good heroin experience at this time?" The "yes" finger lifted and I suggested Lou just enjoy employing his learning and tell me when he had the best of heroin experience. Within a few minutes Lou became flush and said, "this is really good shit". I then asked Lou to touch two fingers together on his non-signaling hand and he did this. Ideomotor confirmation was secured that those two fingers touching would be a physical signal Lou could use at will to develop this same "high".

As Lou enjoyed his experience, I spoke metaphorically of "driving across state lines" and offered ego-strengthening suggestions (Stanton, 1979, 1989, McNeal & Frederick, 1993, Hartland, 1965). As I posed the possibility of his unconscious helping him in various ways to remain free of the urge to use heroin, his "yes" finger lifted in affirmation. Lou was encouraged to write a goodbye letter to his relationship with heroin.

The second session was cancelled by Lou and never rescheduled. I spoke with Lou by phone a month later and he indicated he had remained clean and was using his "best of" tool often and effectively. A year after the session Lou said, by phone, that he wasn't finding as much need to use his "best of" tool as his life seemed to be going well. He had remained free of heroin since our session (case previously cited in Walsh, 2003).

♦

The particular ways in which sufficient concentrations of drugs or alcohol interfere with or skew human to human communication has been observed and documented over the centuries. Not so easy to observe is the way in which communication within the human body is changed by the substances it absorbs.

The communication taking place throughout the body-mind is complex and constant. It involves physiological, intellectual, psychological, perceptual, conscious and unconscious realms of information exchange. Large portions of communication flow best within natural physiological states the body moves through. The various shifting physiological states may be expressed as relaxation, anger, excitement, sexual arousal, anxiety, laughter, joy and more.

Like the communication systems of today which encompass telephone land lines, satellite transmission, computer technology, email, fax and more, communication within the human body-mind is quite involved and multi-dimensional. We will examine a small portion of this communication network directly involved in substance use and substance abuse treatment.

Consider for a moment how a telephone system has millions of users, each with personal identification codes (telephone numbers) and operating systems (telephone companies, type of telephone program and service). There are hardware and software components applied to moving a signal from one location to another and maintaining an open line for two way communication and conference calls. There are signals like mass faxes emanating from a single source, which go to many recipients. Weather conditions sometimes knock out transmission lines, causing information to be rerouted, delayed or undeliverable. Voice mail allows information to be recorded and stored. An unintended recipient sometimes intercepts information. Signals occasionally bleed into other systems and interfere with other communication. Wire taps disperse information further. Information received by one person can be interpreted and then sent to many others in a modified form that alters its meaning. Within the telephone system, information moves along many different paths in many different directions with many possible outcomes.

The body-mind communication network is far more complex than the telephone system. This writing will only scratch the surface of what is now known, for purposes of understanding *Utilization Sobriety* dynamics. Information is always being exchanged within the human psychobiological system. Before examining how drugs and alcohol affect body-mind communication, a superficial look at some basic parts of normal human information processing is in order.

Psycho-neuro-somato-sensory network communication

Our team

The central nervous system (CNS) with its rapid-fire neural transmission is, of course, a key player in all functioning. The CNS relies on charged ions like sodium and potassium to carry electrical signals from one neuron to the next. We could consider the CNS as the bio-hard drive of the human computer with a high degree of plasticity.

The software of the bio-computer is a complex network of molecular information substances. This network runs various programs, maintains a communication loop between organ systems and the CNS and changes physiological states in response to systemic demands or environmental and social circumstances. The software does a remarkable job of adapting, accommodating, maintaining and stabilizing the system it occupies. Persuasive products not native to the system's landscape however, very easily influence it.

All substance introduced into the body has the potential to modify the natural state of the body to varying degrees. It is fitting to mention some of the key "software" components affected by introduced substances. Each component has an interactive relationship with other components. Functional parameters allow one component to transmit information that activates a specific process and outcome.

Nerve cells have many specific molecular interaction sites on their surface. Imagine a cell wall like a wall of lockers at an airport, each locker with a different key combination needed to access its contents. The locks on the locker wall are analogous to cellular receptor sites. Receptors are binding sites for chemicals that instruct cells to start, stop or otherwise regulate various body-mind functions. Receptor sites receive information when a chemical key, called a ligand, fits into the lock. The ligand is part of a messenger molecule or information substance that conveys information to the cell. Each receptor site is coded to match a particular ligand. There are many different types of ligands that fall into three categories.

One type of ligand consists of neurotransmitters. Neurotransmitters carry information across the gap between one nerve cell and the next. This class of ligands includes dopamine, serotonin, anandamide, histamine, norepinephrine, acetylcholine, glycine and GABA (gamma amino-butyric acid).

Steroids make up a second type of ligand. These are hormones like estrogen, progesterone and testosterone that regulate sexual function and expression. Cortisol is another hormone released by the adrenal glands during stressful conditions. Most of the other hormones fall into the next class.

The third category of ligands in composed of a very broad class of compounds called peptides. Peptides are made of strands of amino acids. The particular combination of amino acids in a peptide chain defines its type and function. Their function and point of origin more narrowly define peptides (i.e. where the molecule is manufactured). Peptides produced by nerve cells, for example, are called neuropeptides while peptides born from immune cells are labeled immunopeptides and peptides emitting from the endocrine cells are called hormones. For purposes of this book all peptides will simply be considered *information substances*, a term coined by MIT researcher Francis Schmitt (1986).

The ligand/receptor site communication network can be considered like the software system of our bio-computer. Communication is always happening in this system and very little can happen without it. As with a real computer, the hard drive and software are interdependent and interacting all the time.

Candace Pert (1997) metaphorically compares the ligand/receptor network with another operation. She suggests that if the cell is the engine that drives all of life, then the receptors are the buttons on the control panel of that engine, and a specific ligand is the finger that pushes the button and gets things started.

Pert (1997) describes how ligands associated with particular emotional states have receptor sites not only in high concentration in the limbic region of the brain but on cells of the immune system as well. This could explain much about how physical symptoms develop concurrent with particular emotional states.

Emotional experience

The limbic system is the part of the brain responsible for generating emotion. Key components of the limbic system include the limbic cortex, amygdala, hippocampus and hypothalamus.

The hippocampus is responsible for registering and retrieving emotionally important memories. It compares incoming information to historical experience or information. All recent conscious memories are stored here and those that are destined to become lasting fixtures are dispatched to long-term memory. The hippocampus plays an important role in facilitating new learning.

The amygdala charges sensory information and current perception with emotional cues. It is, among other things, the brain's alarm system. An alarm signal from the amygdala moves to the hypothalamus to quickly generate the primitive fight/flight/freeze response. Anger as well as warm, pleasant feelings are emitted from the amygdala. There is speculation that unconscious memories are stored in the amygdala (LeDoux in Carter, 1999). This suggests that an amygdala-based memory will produce a physical reminiscence, reconstituting the body-state that came about with the original experience. The hippocampus will likewise produce a conscious recollection as an event is recalled.

The amygdala and hippocampus are directly wired to the hypothalamus through which they influence the functioning of the autonomic nervous system and hormonal secretions to regulate physical states and level of arousal. Information about bodily states is constantly fed to the hypothalamus through hormones, neuropeptides and neurotransmitters. Appetite, thirst and other urges originate here. The hypothalamus with the suprachiasmatic nuclei (intersection of optic nerves) calibrates the biological clock.

The peptides associated with various emotions have receptor sites in the central nervous system and the immune system. Emotional experience is systemic and is often an incentive for substance use. Sometimes an emotional expression or awareness is most available only when an individual is invested in a particular substance-state i.e. the angry drunk.

Sometimes a substance-state dulls or obscures emotional experience as it alters the concentration of particular neurotransmitters. This certainly defines the function of a class of antidepressants known as selective serotonin re-uptake inhibitors (SSRI's). As an SSRI creates a state of increased serotonin in the extra-cellular environment, the neurochemistry associated with depression ideally becomes more difficult to maintain.

The emotional information transmitted at a molecular level can have a profound effect on the flow and content of other communication.

Genes

Another set of players we are learning much more about are genes. We do know that many genes are dynamic in their ability to functionally turn on and turn off. Research at this time indicates that social, behavioral and environmental factors seem to play a role in gene expression. Certain gene expression, like that involved in the color of eyes, is static and unchanging. Other gene expression, like that involved in specific disease process, may be quite dynamic. Ernest Rossi (2002) offers an eloquent elaboration on this theme in *The Psychobiology of Gene Expression*.

How might a system wide change in communication and perception (i.e. drug use) influence gene expression? How drug and alcohol use influence gene expression is not at all clear at this time. I can only speculate that habitual use of any substance may establish physiological and environmental circumstances ripe for alterations in gene expression.

State-dependent memory, learning and behavior

The notion that learning, memory and behavior can be encoded or contained within a particular physiological state or biochemical matrix was elucidated through the work of Donald Overton (1971, 1972, 1973, 1982). Overton demonstrated how information coming in from the outer world is responsive to and interactive with the biochemical state of the inner world. Overton (1971) demonstrated how rats, learning a path through a maze under the influence of a certain drug, remember the maze map quickly when exposed to the same drug. Without the drug the rat is more like control rats initially learning the maze. Some information from the outer world may become tightly bound to a particular physiological state and only available to the whole system while in that state. This is called state-dependent memory, learning and behavior.

To illustrate this phenomenon I reference a clinical case. A woman could not remember where she had hidden some money. She reported having indulged in the drug known as ecstasy (methylenedioxymethamphetamine) around the time the money was hidden. After establishing sufficient safety and securing an adequate context for hypnosis, the woman developed a trance. In trance she imagined taking ecstasy. After she reported having the felt experience of ecstasy, I reflected information she had shared about time and place. I asked where she hid the money. The memory surfaced quickly. The memory, I speculate, was likely held or encoded in the physiological state induced by ecstasy. This ecstasy-state was then accessed via communication with the unconscious mind. Desired information surfaced readily.

Consider some of the physiological "states" we move in and out of every day. When we are relaxed and comfortable without any additives like alcohol, our brain chemistry may reflect elevated serotonin levels. When we are excited about doing something thrilling, our physiological state is likely biased in favor of dopamine. When we are sexually aroused, our inner environment is richly interwoven with sex hormones. When we are anxious, the adrenal glands contribute much to this characteristic state.

Ernest Rossi (1988) proposes a concise model for state-dependent phenomena which I will paraphrase here: Neuronal networks in the brain are activated by information substances. Information is transmitted to a nerve cell that incites a biochemical chain of events. Information substances in these neuronal networks encode state-dependent memory, learning and behavior. Information substances modulate the molecular-genetic basis of memory, learning and behavior. The information substance/receptor communication systems are the psychobiological basis of state-dependent body-mind experience.

Ligands and receptor sites

A handful of ligands and receptor sites specifically affected by substances coming from outside the body need some elucidation here.

• The neurotransmitter **dopamine** plays a significant role in both normal, healthy life and in substance dependence. Dopamine is very involved in the regulation of mood and affect because it plays a primary part in the processes of motivation and reward. It also helps regulate fine motor activity, satiation and emotional stability. Dopamine interacts with neurons at a number of different dopamine receptor sites. Major depression is associated with a deficiency of dopamine in the limbic system of the brain (Klimek et al, 2002). Excess dopamine causes many of the effects of schizophrenia (Inaba & Cohen, 2004). Parkinson's disease destroys dopamine-producing areas of the brain.

Different people have different baseline levels of dopamine under normal circumstances. Neurons in the limbic system of the brain regularly release low levels of dopamine. Since the limbic system is very involved with mood and emotional experience, these low levels of dopamine may establish a baseline biochemical state responsible for maintaining normal affect and mood. This neurotransmitter affects brain processes that control movement, emotional response and ability to experience pleasure and pain. The dopamine system is important to positive reinforcement, drive and motivation. This molecule is quite crucial for mental and physical health.

- **Serotonin** is a neurotransmitter that acts as a mellowing agent in many ways. It is involved in regulation of emotions, appetite, anxiety, sleep, stress hormones and other body functions. Serotonin inhibits neuronal activity in the amygdala and modulates transmission of emotionally salient information from the sensory cortices to the amygdala. Serotonin engages neurons at serotonin receptor sites. Very low levels of serotonin are observed in people with major depression (Schloss & Williams, 1998).

- **Anandamide** is a neurotransmitter with ligand functionality at cannabinoid receptor sites. It is an endogenous cannabinoid with very similar properties to the main psychoactive ingredient found in marijuana, tetrahydrocannabinol (THC). Anandamide is thought to play a role in pain, depression, appetite, memory and fertility (Randall, 2003). It is found in the limbic system and the areas of the brain responsible for integration of sensory experiences with emotions as well as those areas controlling learning, motor coordination and memory. Anandamide is believed to inhibit or limit the formation of short-term memory during the sleep cycle.

- Another molecular player affected by drug and alcohol use is a class of chemicals known as **endogenous opioids**. This class includes **endorphins** and **enkaphalins**. These are feel-good molecules released by neurons when the body is in pain or stress. Endorphins can create an analgesic effect by crowding the space between neurons and inhibiting the firing of nerve cells. Endorphins can also have an excitatory effect and allow us to feel good, euphoric and free from pain. Endorphins interact at the neuronal endorphin receptor sites. Endorphin levels typically go up as a person exercises, goes into labor or experiences stress. Endorphins have been found in emotionally generated tears (i.e. tears of grief, tears of joy) but not in chemically generated tears (i.e. cutting onions) (Frey et al, 1981).

We now know that both the CNS and the immune system produce endorphins (Ruff & Pert, 1986; Pert, 1997; Ader, Felten & Cohen, 1991). These peptides bind to the same cell receptor sites as do heroin, morphine and similar drugs. We know that endorphins are released in response to situational and environmental demands (Brown, 1991; van der Kolk, Pitman, Orr & Greenberg, 1989). Endorphins of various classes are involved in stress response, immune function, reproductive biology, gastrointestinal function, cardiovascular status, mood change and response to pain (Kreek, 1998).

- **GABA-A**, gamma-aminobutyric acid A-type, is an inhibitory neurotransmitter involved in the gating of ion channels that influence electrical conduction. Its effects can be sedating and paradoxically behaviorally disinhibiting. GABA is thought to limit neuronal activity in areas of the brain associated with panic. GABA receptor sites potentiate GABA functioning. Research indicates that low levels of GABA function may lead to increased anxiety and anxiety is reduced when GABA function is increased. GABA acts to reduce the firing of dopamine producing cells (Maitra & Reynolds, 1998).

- **Glutamate** is an excitatory neurotransmitter thought to play a major role in learning and memory, as well as motor function and sensory function. Glutamate receptor sites are involved in the gating of ion channels that influence electrical conduction in the nervous system.

- **Acetylcholine** is an excitatory neurotransmitter that plays a critical role in chemical signaling throughout the nervous system. It helps control mental acuity, memory and learning. Acetylcholine generally has a stimulating effect on muscle tissue, but in the circulatory system it causes vasodilation and decreased blood pressure. When acetylcholine occupies the nicotinic receptor site, one of a number of acetylcholine receptor sites, electrical conductance of the neuron is enhanced (Fryer & Lukas, 1999). This molecule is thought to be overactive in major depression and deficient in Alzheimer's disease (Martin-Ruiz et al, 1999)).

- **Norepinephrine** (also known as noradrenaline), released from the adrenal gland, is an energizing neurotransporter derived from dopamine. It is released when the body demands more energy. It plays a significant role in the fight, flight or freeze response and in memory formation, motivation, hunger, attention span and alertness. Insufficient levels of norepinephrine may result in low energy and depression, while excess contributes to anxiety, vasoconstriction, increased heart rate and blood pressure. A moderate amount of this neurotransmitter amplifies feelings of well being.

Psychobiological dynamics with substance

The other team

A number of problem substances exert their influence by commandeering or persuading natural ligand and receptor site functions. A number of substance categories listed here illustrate very briefly how some of the commandeering is done. Each substance category, including opiates, alcohol, amphetamines, nicotine, barbiturates, cocaine, benzodiazepines and cannabis, engages a somewhat different physiological mechanism outlined in Chart 1.

- **Cocaine** functions to prevent the reuptake or absorption of extra-cellular dopamine by binding to the proteins that normally transport dopamine. This causes levels of dopamine to increase in the environment surrounding neurons, stimulating neurons and producing feelings of pleasure and excitement. Cocaine also blocks the uptake of serotonin and norepinephrine (Hall et al, 2002). Prolonged use of cocaine over-stimulates and desensitizes nerve cells to create tolerance. Tolerance, of course, prompts more intense drug usage.

- **Amphetamine** also causes an increase in extra-cellular

dopamine, but in a slightly different manner than cocaine. Amphetamine stimulates the release of more dopamine from the cells it affects. As an agonist or promoter of norepinephrine and serotonin, it facilitates increased concentration of these neurotransmitters in the extracellular environment. Other dynamics resulting in drug tolerance are similar to cocaine and related stimulants.

- **Heroin** and other **opioid derivatives** like opium, hydromorphone, codeine and morphine increase the activity rate of dopamine producing cells by fitting into a cell's endorphin or enkephalin receptor sites, also known as opioid receptor sites. Opioids also switch off the firing of GABA neurons that inhibit the dopamine cell firing. This increased activity in dopamine cells causes the cells to release more dopamine and produce mood elevation and feelings of euphoria. The affective experience reinforces motivation for repetition.

- **Heroin and cocaine** combined (known as a "speedball") produce a powerful and dangerous jolt because of the different ways they engage the dopamine system. Heroin increases the activity or firing of cells and increases the release of dopamine. Cocaine holds the released dopamine in the extra-cellular environment longer and thereby magnifies and extends its effects.

- **Alcohol** substitutes itself for neurotransmitters at the receptor sites for GABA-A and endorphins, causing the release of endorphins. Endogenous opioid receptor sites are involved in appetite, pain and response to stress.

Alcohol also blocks the neurotransmitter glutamate (an excitatory amino acid).

- **Marijuana** contains the psychoactive ingredient tetrahydrocannabinol (THC) which interfaces with the receptor site for a lipid neurotransmitter called anandamide. The pharmacological activity of THC may be partially mediated by serotonin receptors and play a role in regulating dopamine transmission.

- **Benzodiazepines** act upon the GABA-A receptor sites by impersonating GABA-A. Typically, the binding of benzodiazepines increases the GABA receptor sites' affinity for GABA.

- **Nicotine** acts upon nicotinic acetylcholine receptor sites which affect skeletal and heart muscle function, among other things. (Fryer & Lucas, 1999)

- **Ecstasy** (MDMA- methylenedioxymethamphetamine) functions to increase the release of serotonin and dopamine. MDMA has been found to damage serotonin-producing neurons (NIDA 1996).

- **PCP** (phencyclidine, also known as **angel dust**) and **ketamine** produce a dissociative affect by influencing the functions of most of the neurotransmitters discussed thus far. Many receptor sites fall under the influence of these drugs.

- **LSD** functions at a number of serotonin receptor sites. LSD also interacts with dopamine receptors and has a unique capacity for modulating dopamine transmission. Other psychedelics like mescaline and psilocybin also operate at serotonin receptor sites.

- **Barbiturates** block the release of glutamate and thus enhance the neural inhibition function of GABA. As GABA agonists, barbiturates serve a sedating, hypnotic purpose.

This list is not comprehensive and represents only a portion of the substances being used by people today. The biochemical mechanisms illustrated here seem to support one path by which the *Utilization Sobriety* method may achieve effective results.

Chart 1.

Substance	Ligand affected	Neuroreceptor site
Cocaine	dopamine, serotonin norepinephrine	dopamine
Amphetamine	dopamine, serotonin norepinephrine	dopamine
Opioid derivatives	endorphins, GABA, dopamine	opioid
Alcohol	GABA, endorphins	GABA, opioid
Benzodiazapines	GABA	GABA
Marijuana	anandamide	cannabinoid
Ecstasy (MDMA)	serotonin, dopamine	serotonin, dopamine
Angel dust (PCP)	most neurotransmitters	many sites
Ketamine	most neurotransmitters	many sites
LSD	serotonin	serotonin
Barbiturates	glutamate	glutamate
Nicotine	acetylcholine	nicotinic acetylcholine

A natural, quite sophisticated and fully functional endogenous pharmaceutical system is the backdrop against which any drug or alcohol use begins. The natural system can certainly be damaged to various degrees by external substances.

We also know that the extra-cellular and intracellular flow of neurotransmitters like dopamine and serotonin, can be regulated quite naturally or with the addition of various substances, whether a prescribed medication or illicit drug (Crenshaw & Goldberg, 1996; Brown, 1991; PDR, 2005). Intake of any psychotropic substance creates an ecological shift in which the normal flow of molecular communication (neurotransmitters, peptides) is altered (Pert et al, 1985; Pert, 1997). This is seen as a benefit, for instance, when the "normal" state of experience is depression and an SSRI (selective serotonin re-uptake inhibitor) medication blocks particular cellular receptor cites to favorably change the chemical environment and mood (PDR, 2005).

We have taken a very cursory glimpse at pieces of body-mind communication related to drug use and drug use treatment. We identified some of the hardware and software of the human psycho-neuro-somato-sensory network that fluidly develops, engages and communicates within various physiological states.

Communication is always taking place as information substances or ligands interact with receptor sites. State-dependent memory, learning and behavior are encoded into nerve cells through neuronal information substances. An overview of the limbic system poses a backdrop for the emotional components of substance use, substance withdrawal and motivation for change. Questions are raised about the potential influence of substance use on gene expression. The specific ways some substances mimic or undermine natural receptor site ligand communication has broad implications concerning state-dependent learning, memory and behavior.

◆

This discussion about body-mind communication points to the potential benefit of exploring types of person to person communication that allow access to various physiological states and/or their experiential counterpart. Might this discussion about internal states and information substances involved in those states suggest benefit in accessing both memory of a state and memories within a state?

Chapter five

Evidence of Other Intelligence Within-Developing Ideomotor Signals

In terms of energy, polarity means potential, and wherever a potential exists there is the possibility of a current, a flow of events, for the tension of opposites strives for balance.
Carl Jung, 1959

What if I ... shared a story?

For instance: Nori was the oldest child in a close knit, fatherless, poor inner city family. As a young responsible adult, she left home and began to pursue her occupational goals. Nori's mother held the family together and when she died suddenly, the weight of her loss almost crushed Nori. She tried to hold things together with the family, and work her job and find care for the younger siblings. As social agencies became involved and Nori saw the younger kids placed in homes, she returned to the apartment she shared with a former coworker. The coworker saw enormous pain and distress in Nori and offered some relief.

Nori initially thought the heroin was a passing gift to help her through the grief, nothing she would spend money on or become dependent on. She succumbed to heroin for two years before seeking help at a methadone clinic, the only treatment she believed she could afford.

As Nori found herself doing a balancing act between shifting concentrations of heroin and methadone, she made some phone calls to investigate alternate treatment. She really wanted to get on with her life drug free, and was motivated to find something that worked.

She came to our appointment with desire for change, but little hope. She complied with my request not use heroin or methadone after the afternoon dose of the day before. With expected withdrawal symptoms, she was not looking good throughout the first part of our session. As Nori reluctantly spoke to the benefits she derived from the heroin experience, her tearful story unfolded. She concluded it was better to face the pain and get on with her life than to cover it over with a drug, even a prescribed medication like methadone.

Nori retrieved the best aspects of the heroin experience to her satisfaction without any drug. She developed what I call a benefit state tool that allowed her to call up the same drug-free experience as desired. Nori looked and reported feeling better than she had at the beginning of our session.

Even at a reduced fee, Nori said she couldn't afford more treatment for a while. A six-month follow up call on my part found Nori doing well. She did not, however, remain well after leaving my office. With some reported embarrassment, Nori said, "I thought it was hypnosis or something I didn't understand at all that brought me relief in your office. I was sure I couldn't do that on my own so I used. After a month, I remembered your words when I was getting ready to use and figured I had nothing to lose by trying that heroin tool. It worked; still works and I've been clean since. I got rid of that roommate."

A one year follow up call found Nori making progress with her occupational pursuits, still drug free and using her benefit state tool less often.

•

You are probably aware of how the unconscious mind is expressing itself all the time. It only takes watching two people engaged in a conversation. Heads shake and nod as faces contort in both odd and common ways. Posture changes as hands flail about. Could this event possibly be choreographed, rehearsed and performed with such precision and uncanny cadence by two individuals not at all versed in the ways of theater? The unmistakable spontaneity counters suspicion of rehearsal. Is it not the dance of conscious and unconscious expression? Sometimes body language and intentional verbal presentation pace each other in perfect harmony. Or sometimes the body speaks what the voice does not, untethered to polite convention. People commonly shake or nod their heads to affirm "yes" or "no" in conjunction with other posturing. The head movements and posturing are not typically premeditated and do typically reflect unconscious communication. It just happens automatically. You can work with this same principle to develop a signaling system with the unconscious mind employing fingers.

Why not utilize the language the unconscious speaks so well and add a few words to it? Body language is well established and usually quite understandable to the receptive observer. You really can communicate directly with the unconscious using a particular form of body language. This facilitates dialogue with the unconscious network that has custodial oversight of so many helpful resources. This unconscious intelligence is aware of what is happening in the body and sometimes quite persuasive about changing somatic conditions. It is aware of personal experiential history with related learning and emotion. It is a conduit to various states holding state-dependent learning, memory and behavior.

The body language of which I speak is *ideomotor signaling* or ideomotor questioning, originally derived from hypnotic protocol. Some prefer to define this communication as *ideodynamic signaling*. No hypnotic induction or expertise in hypnosis is required to conduct ideomotor questioning. Some understanding of hypnotic phenomena (i.e. hallucination, time distortion, amnesia, hypermnesia or vivid recall, catalepsy, dissociation- Edgette, 1995) and familiarity with hypnotic protocol is helpful, of course, but not essential for applying this method.

Ideomotor questioning provides a convenient means of accessing and utilizing sensory, emotional, cognitive and physiological learning without needing to navigate through perceptual limitations. During the *Utilization Sobriety* procedure, ideomotor facility allows for a seamless transition to treatment of co-morbid themes which may be contributing or precipitating factors of substance use (Cheek, 1994; Cheek & LeCron, 1968; Rossi, 1986; Walsh, 1997). Ideomotor questioning can provide information helpful in identifying therapeutic priorities and direction, *regardless of what treatment approach is subsequently applied*. Ideomotor questioning and the *Utilization Sobriety* integrate nicely into other treatment modalities and orientations.

Soliciting the unconscious to lift one finger for a "yes" signal and a different finger for a "no" signal allows for very direct communication with the unconscious. Once the signals are established, questions geared for a yes or no answer can be presented to the unconscious and a response secured. This allows access to past learning on many different levels - learning that can be applied beneficially.

Involuntary movements may develop in parts of the body other than the fingers when yes and no signals are requested. These other movements can usually be converted to finger movements or simply employed as they are. These variations are explored later in this chapter.

Some people are more inclined to experience unconscious expression in a somatosensory form. These people may feel a distinct sensation in a finger or somewhere else in place of movement or before movement occurs. The sensation might be a tingling, pressure, numbness, heat, cold, a sharp jolt or something else. This is called *ideosensory signaling* and will be illustrated later in this chapter.

The person who experiences distinct sensation in a finger without involuntary movement of that finger can be encouraged to intentionally lift the finger experiencing the sensation.

During treatment questioning, naturally occurring responses such as a head nod may take place simultaneous with developed finger signals. Erickson (Erickson et al, 1976) commonly worked with a client's ideomotor expression and solicited responses via physical movement. Others have elaborated on the development of specific ideomotor signals and approaches to questioning unconscious process (Cheek & LeCron, 1968; Cheek, 1994; Rossi & Cheek, 1988; Rossi, 1986, 1993).

Box One contains a three-step approach to developing ideomotor signals.

The unconscious signal may seem slow to develop or express itself more as a vibration or side to side movement. All that really matters is that there is a visible movement representing an unconscious response.

Box 1.
Developing Ideomotor Finger Signals

Offer a client the following instructions (a variation on Rossi & Cheek, 1988):

♦ "You have an unconscious (subconscious, inner) mind that is expressing itself all the time through head nods and shakes and hand movements without conscious intention. Its primary purpose is to help you. You can let it help you and even access inner resources by allowing the unconscious to communicate through your fingers. One finger can lift up as a "yes" signal from the unconscious and a different finger can lift up as a "no" signal."

♦ "Position yourself comfortably so your fingers are not impeded in any way. Let yourself focus on something very positive, thinking and feeling 'yes, yes, yes'. It may be a place you like, a favorite activity, a nice memory or something else. As you focus on that positive theme, one of those fingers can lift up all by itself as a "yes" signal from the unconscious. * Think of yourself as a curious observer, as you really don't know which of those fingers is going to lift up. The eyes can be open or closed. The unconscious mind has all the time necessary to develop that signal. (Acknowledge the establishment of a "yes" signal after witnessing a finger lift up or vibrate in a noticeable manner.)

♦ Now that we have a "yes" signal, that "yes" finger can rest. You might wonder which other finger on that same hand will lift up as a "no" signal. Let yourself focus on something representing "no"- an alarm clock going off, a flat tire, a bad taste or anything negative, thinking and feeling 'no, no, no'. As the unconscious determines which finger is appropriate for a "no" signal, that finger will float up easily. If you have any difficulty holding a particular theme, imagine seeing the word "no" in big bold letters. (Acknowledge the establishment of a "no" signal after seeing a finger lift or vibrate.) Unconscious finger movements are typically a bit different than consciously directed movement.

* (Optional: "You may feel distinct sensations in a finger or hand

> even before a finger moves. Or you may feel nothing at all as a finger lifts up. There are many variations to this experience with no right or wrong way. If you are having any difficulty developing a single positive theme, just imagine seeing the word "yes" in big, bold letters.")

I will embellish this procedure in a somewhat repetitive fashion with the following instructions for the therapist.

1. First ask the client if it is acceptable to develop a signaling system with that helpful intelligence within, the unconscious mind. Then ask the client, sitting in a comfortable position, to position his or her hands, palms up or down, in a way that allows all fingers to move freely. Begin scanning the hands for any movement as you suggest the client focus on something positive. The focus may be a favorite activity or food, a special place, a fond memory or anything striking a positive note for the client. Indicate how, as that positive focus is maintained, a finger will lift up as a clear, visible "yes" signal from the unconscious. Assure the client that the unconscious has all the time it needs to develop that "yes" signal. I like to thank the unconscious for being so responsive after a signal is established.

2. After securing a "yes" signal, suggest that the "yes" finger can now rest. Infer that the client might wonder which other finger on that same hand will lift up as a "no" signal from the unconscious. Ask the client to focus on something that represents "no", thinking and feeling no, no, no as a different finger on that same hand lifts

up to signal "no". After the "no" signal is established, you are free to ask questions of the unconscious.

3. I like to ratify the signals, when not using the *Utilization Sobriety* approach, by asking "Is it alright to call up a deep experience of comfort and calm for your benefit at this time?" A "yes" or "no" response will ratify the signals. A "yes" response may be followed by some encouragement to enjoy the process. As will be explained in the next chapter, ratification of the ideomotor signals during the US procedure requests something other than comfort and calm.

There are many variations concerning how ideomotor signals are expressed. The fingers of the person you are working with may lift up or move distinctly as requested or expected. Unconscious movements, however, are typically not as dynamic or rapid as conscious movements. The unconscious signal in a finger usually begins as a slight vibration or twitch, a very subtle movement. The vibration may evolve into a fully extended or elevated finger. The vibration may produce a saccadic, side to side motion. The twitch may never go beyond a twitch. In some people, unconscious finger movements may closely resemble volitional, conscious movements.

Sometimes fingers group in twos or threes to produce a signal. The index finger and thumb might move as a "yes" signal while the ring and pinky fingers move simultaneously as a "no" signal.

Sometimes a signaling finger will seem to raise the entire hand, causing involuntary hand levitation. This, as all ideomotor responses, can be validated and utilized. You might suggest "Yes, that is a very clear, strong signal and there may be much more for me to learn from that response. It really is OK to just let a finger communicate that (yes or no) signal if you like."

In spite of what is requested or suggested, yes and no signals may develop on different hands or have complementary signals on opposing hands. In other words, the unconscious can always exercise its creative license when it responds. All that is important is getting a response from the unconscious.

To complicate matters more, an ideomotor signal may develop in a part of the body other than the hands. The unconscious is creative and can respond to questions and suggestions in ways we don't normally expect. A man I worked with developed a yes signal with an index finger quite readily. The "no" signal did not seem to be forthcoming until I paid attention to what I was dismissing as a peculiar mannerism. This man's left eyebrow lifted up to signal "no".

Another person who presented wearing sandals without socks produced yes and no signals with the movement of right and left big toes. In this case, and the eyebrow case, the unconscious agreed to expand the signaling repertoire by adding appropriate finger signals to the other selected form of communicating. The original signals were first acknowledged and appreciated before requesting additional signals solely for my convenience. If the sandal-clad person came to a session wearing shoes and socks, there would be some obvious limitations for ideomotor communication if something else had not been developed for signaling.

The most important factor when developing ideomotor signals is observation. Most of the time signals will develop in fingers. Very subtle head nodding or shaking may also accompany respective finger signals. Yes and no finger signals on one hand is what I prefer because this narrows the range of observation necessary by the clinician and frees the other hand for other purposes. I believe this one handed signaling also simplifies effective communication for the unconscious mind.

As you solicit finger signals be very patient to see what develops. Assume that something will indeed happen. It is common for the person developing finger signals to become impatient and assume the process is not working or a personal failure has occurred. Assure the person it is a personal experience and absolutely impossible to do wrong. Encourage the person to continue focussing on the positive or negative theme and be curious about what happens.

For people who say they cannot produce a single positive image or thought, suggest they simply imagine seeing the word "yes" in big block letters, nothing more. The same would apply conversely for a "no" signal. This approach frequently produces quick results and reduces performance anxiety.

Another somewhat paradoxical approach for the person unable to conjure up a single positive thing for the "yes" signal involves suggesting "perhaps thinking of saying 'no' is something positive for you."

If three or four minutes pass without observing any noticeable movement, ask the client about his or her experience. "What are you aware of right now?" Frame the non-response as "This may be what needs to happen to develop this style of communication for you."

Variations in responses may reflect creative play, metaphoric communication, a personality style/trait, an attempt to confuse the observer, mistrust of the therapist, a test and more. Any conjecture may or may not be accurate and could be investigated for the sake of analysis. All that is really important is establishing clear communication with the unconscious.

For most people, the ideomotor signals remain constant once they are established. Take note, for future reference, of which fingers or other movements represent yes and no signals. I have encountered a few people, however, whose signals changed visit to visit during the early phase of treatment. I asked for yes and no finger signal confirmation at the beginning of each session. The signals usually remained consistent throughout each session. I couldn't resist drawing conclusions about the psychodynamics of why this session to session inconsistency was happening. I never confronted the clients about this except in a humorous, normalizing, reflective manner. In each case, the signals eventually became consistent and the clients volunteered information which offered explanations about the signal switching.

Ideosensory Signals

A few words about ideosensory communication are in order. The unconscious often communicates or expresses itself through a sensory experience. Likewise, a sensory experience can easily and rapidly trigger the unconscious to retrieve a memory involving that particular sense experience. A woman walks in with the scent of perfume and suddenly I'm transported back in time, getting a smothering kiss from Aunt Elma after Sunday school. Sometimes we have what has been called a *body memory* as we feel a sensation surfacing from a past experience. We may also develop a twitch or tick as we focus on a particular thought or circumstance.

Yes and no ideosensory signals can be developed intentionally as with ideomotor signals. Sometimes, however, ideosensory responses develop in place of or simultaneous to ideomotor signals. For this reason it is always good to ask about the client's experience. Substitution of unsolicited ideosensory for ideomotor signals is rare in my experience, but well worth being aware of.

Ideosensory signaling requires verbal feedback from your client. The following example illustrates one instance of ideosensory communication. Mary had been working on some family of origin issues but was distracted by a persistent pain in her back. She said she had been to the doctor the same day and the doctor found nothing remarkable. Mary was irritated with the doctor's dismissal of her pain and asked if I thought it could just be in her head. I told her I had no idea what was causing the pain but the pain itself might help her understand more. Mary wanted to pursue this.

I suggested that Mary's system could respond to questions by increasing the pain for "yes" and decreasing the pain for "no". I asked Mary to imagine the pain sensation on a zero to ten scale so she could numerically report changes.

I (hereafter designated as "B") began the questioning by first asking "Is this type of questioning acceptable for the unconscious?". Mary (hereafter designated as "M") then felt a jolt of pain in her back and assumed the answer to my question was yes.

B "Is it alright to understand the source of the back pain you have been experiencing?".

M "The pain increased."

B "Is the source of this pain related to a prior experience in which you were injured?"

M "The pain lessened."

B "Is the source of this pain related in any way to

emotional containment?"

M "The pain went down again."

B "Is the source of this pain something requiring medical attention?"

M "It went up to a seven."

B "Is there an ongoing physical condition requiring medical attention?"

M "It got worse."

B "Assuming Mary will get medical attention for this condition, is it alright for Mary to understand more about the source of this pain?"

M "That was a yes."

Mary remained quiet with eyes closed for a few minutes. Her face then became flush and she said "Oh, that's it. It's my left ovary. I just got a piece of this dream I had involving the left ovary."

Mary made another doctor appointment and more testing revealed a growth on her left ovary. The condition was treated effectively without surgery.

In this case I utilized a symptom to establish ideosensory signals. I earlier spoke of ideosensory signals automatically developing in place of or in conjunction with ideomotor signals. This example illustrates the reality of ideosensory communication from the unconscious and demonstrates the ease with which it can be employed with a person willing and able to communicate verbally. Mary also was willing to tolerate the discomfort of communicating through a pain medium.

Ideosensory communication doesn't require the presence of pain. Any distinct sensation from any of the senses can be employed.

♦

Ideomotor questioning is a simple, effective means of communicating with the unconscious mind. The method is easily learned and applied. Developing this option for communication with the unconscious affords the client much more control, as they are able to access so much more of themselves. There are many possible variations regarding how the unconscious develops signals. Ideosensory questioning is another variation on unconscious communication not typically solicited for the *Utilization Sobriety* procedure. The next chapter describes how ideomotor questioning is applied within the context of the full *Utilization Sobriety* procedure.

Chapter Six

The Utilization Sobriety Method

Who never doubted, never half believed. Where doubt is, there truth is. It is her shadow.
Gamaleil Bailey

No formal trance induction is needed in the *Utilization Sobriety* procedure, also referenced as US. Although developing ideomotor finger signals may produce various levels of trance, it is only the establishment of the signals that is necessary for the treatment to be engaged. Questions are posed in a way that allows the subject's peculiar needs to determine the development and depth of trance, should it occur.

The experiential insulation resulting from substance use (hypothesized as an adaptive/protective function) is accommodated in a client-empowering way that supports adjustments to healthy choice. This accommodation is addressed early in treatment to acknowledge any perceived need being served by substance use, thus maintaining client integrity. Validating client attempts to satisfy honest needs also normalizes the ambivalence so commonly a part of substance abuse treatment.

The *Utilization Sobriety* protocol calls for ample client preparation for unconscious work and the establishment of good rapport. This may involve providing information about unconscious process and functioning, referencing enhanced client control as inner resources are accessed, eliciting client's picture of a goal achieved and discussing possible awkwardness adjusting to the change. Once adequate preparation has taken place, proceed as outlined in Box 2.

Box 2.

Utilization Sobriety

1. Obtain a substance use history. Solicit information about client's current life circumstances.

2. Elicit and note words which describe any perceived benefit (emotional, intellectual, sensory, perceptual, behavioral, social etc.) of substance use for client.

3. Ask client "If it were possible, would you like to be able to experience the same benefits you derive from using X without actually using X?" If the response is affirmative, then provide more information about the unconscious access to stored memory of experience (behavioral, emotional, physiological etc.). Explain how the physiological system learned all about X after its first usage and how learning can be retrieved and used for client's benefit.

4. Suggest accessing useful learning by opening a simple channel to the unconscious. Explain how ideomotor finger signals work and how the client will remain in full control as help is obtained from unconscious resources.

5. Develop "yes" and "no" ideomotor finger signals as described in Chapter Five.

6. Help client retrieve the best parts of the substance use state via ideomotor questioning and verification. Asking "Is it alright at this time to call up the very best aspects of X use that you described to me earlier? (Review terms client used to describe benefits)." If the "yes" finger lifts, say "So that can now happen. When you really have the best of the X experience, that 'yes' finger can lift up as a signal." Encourage client to tell you when he or she feels the change. If the "no" finger lifts, investigate higher priorities or obstacles via ideomotor questioning.

7. While client is experiencing the "benefit" state, develop a physical signal (hereafter called the benefit state tool or BST) that client can use at will to develop this state. Anchor the experience to two fingers touching or the squeeze of an ear lobe or something else. Secure ideomotor confirmation that the anchoring signal will retrieve the "benefit" state. Suggest the client can access this state by putting in a request for the benefit-state to the unconscious and employing the physical signal. Elaborate on how the BST is there to use any time, any place. Test the signal before the session ends. Encourage the client to practice using the benefit state tool any time he or she is tempted to use the actual substance or involved in stressful circumstances.

8. Client is informed of the significant adjustment involved in changing any relationship. Since the client's relationship with the substance of choice is changing, the client is asked to write a goodbye letter to this relationship. The letter should be complete in addressing all significant elements of the relationship (i.e. the purpose it served, benefits and detriments, associations with the substance, learning, influences etc.) and the anticipated components of grief. Client is encouraged to keep a journal about changes and to focus on self-care as it relates to exercise, nutrition, social involvement and rest.

Caution: When working with those previously involved in substance abuse treatment programs or 12 step programs, it is sometimes prudent to avoid language that may associate the benefit/substance-state with the substance. Cognitive congruence may be maintained by presenting the benefit-state as a natural, healthy realization of potentials that were present prior to substance involvement.

Subsequent sessions may focus on reinforcing client gains, relapse prevention strategies, addressing other mental health needs or whatever is inimitably most relevant to the client's concerns.

Intention

The intention of the *Utilization Sobriety* procedure is multifaceted and, as outlined in Chapter Two, aims to:

- Idiosyncratically utilize the client's psychobiological system, simply by asking for an experience.
- Affirm and empower clients to enhance self-esteem, as personal power and control are exercised.
- Incorporate a mechanism for relapse prevention, as the benefit state tool is available all the time.
- Foster change without eliminating coping strategies employed by the client, using just the best elements of a substance experience with an inner locus of control.
- Provide a safe foundation for addressing the client's mental health themes related to substance misuse, without segregating substance abuse from mental health, using a direct channel of communication with the unconscious.

Sobriety is the ultimate goal. By way of achieving this goal, there is the intention of eliciting the psychobiological mechanism (learning or memory) which previously responded to personal needs through substance use. Eliciting this response to the needs mechanism then allows for rapid withdrawal and sobriety.

Successfully completing the withdrawal process and maintaining sobriety involves harnessing the *response to needs* mechanism for willful use as desired by the individual in treatment. This speaks to a second facet of intention that establishes an internal locus of control regarding dependency themes. The previous dependence on a substance defined an external locus of control.

Harnessing the response to needs mechanism or, as defined in the US procedure, developing the *benefit state tool* (BST) thus creates a sense of mastery over the addiction process. A sense of mastery, as Bandura (1977) says, is an essential component of self-esteem.

The US method intends to work with the individual's system, not against it. A therapist, acknowledging the presence of valid needs that demand attention or amelioration, strengthens rapport and somewhat normalizes any subsequent attempt to address very real needs.

The procedure described here is what seems to work best with the majority of people I treat. Circumstances may demand creative applications or interpretations of the principles supporting this approach. There have been many variations in my own practice. Exploring variations on other themes is how the US approach evolved. In other words, there is no need to be fundamentalist about all the details suggested here. The overriding principles are important but there is much room for variation within those principles.

Before starting US procedure

Some degree of separation from the substance in question is necessary for this procedure to work effectively. Twenty-four hours abstinence from the substance is ideal and what I recommend most of the time. Twelve hours abstinence is acceptable when seriously physiologically addictive substances like heroin are involved or when alcohol dependence requires significant daily maintenance dosing.

The *Utilization Sobriety* approach solicits the experiential emergence of key components integral to a substance-state. If a person is already actively involved in the substance-state, it makes no sense to request the development of that state. Unwittingly attempting to create what already exists may insult the unconscious mind of the client and sabotage further progress.

A person must recognize some favorable experiential contrast in order for this treatment to seed change. Many times I have rescheduled appointments for the US intervention after recognizing a person was still under the influence of a target substance. At the beginning of a session it is always important to inquire about the most recent use of the substance in question or any other substance that could have a bearing on the treatment procedure. Explain to the client how an important window of opportunity is created by the prescribed period of abstinence. Most people who are motivated to make a change will be honest about the last substance indulgence. Some will lie and confound treatment.

Step One - Obtaining substance use history

The first step in this treatment involves gathering information about substance use history and current life circumstances. This not only gives you useful information about client experience, but tells you about client language, style of presentation, affect, motivation, underlying themes likely relevant to sobriety challenges and more. As questions are posed in a very non-judgmental manner, a fluid, responsive relational field forms more easily.

I typically begin a session by saying to the client "My job is not about making judgments concerning you or your experience. Casting judgment doesn't serve any purpose for you or me. My job is about exploring possibilities to help you get where you want to be."

Questions about the history of substance use might sound like the following: When were you first introduced to X (substance in question)? What was the relationship with X like in the beginning and how did it change over time? Did you attempt to end the relationship at times? What got in the way of ending the relationship? How often and how much do you use X? Have you been able to be away from X for the past 24 hours? What is your physical experience like right now? What are your feelings about ending the relationship now? What are your thoughts about ending the relationship now? In spite of whatever fight you think X might provoke to keep the relationship going, please tell me what your experience will look like (be like, feel like) as you imagine winning independence from X? What will others notice about you, even if they don't know you're free of X?

The last few questions are an attempt to seed a change picture or perceptual possibility without the weight of expectation or promise of cure. This type of seeding was a common theme in the work of Milton Erickson (1976) and is the cornerstone of solution focussed therapy (deShazer, 1988).

Questions about current life circumstances might go something like this: How was it for you getting to this appointment today? Since we just met, will you help me understand what a usual day is like for you? Are weekdays different than weekends? What is your living situation like? Live alone or with others? How do you typically spend your time? What do you enjoy doing, now or in the past? Is there anything you anticipate getting in the way of your work here, today or in the future?

Much of the inquiry is quite similar to and compatible with an approach called *Motivational Interviewing* (Miller & Rollnick, 1991). This mode of questioning aims to gather information while establishing a therapeutic relationship and enhancing motivation. Motivational Interviewing will be discussed further in Chapter Nine.

Some degree of ambivalence about substance use and its treatment is, of course, common for most people in treatment. Direct or indirect non-judgmental acknowledgement of the ambivalence normalizes this dynamic and usually complements the therapeutic relationship. The next step curiously embraces this notion.

Step Two - Perceived benefits of substance use

Information gathering leads smoothly to coaxing words from the client that define the benefits of substance use. Many people, when asked about substance use benefits, will display a very black and white response by saying "there is nothing good about it- its ruining my life!" , or some variation on that theme. It usually takes persistence on the part of the provider to access information about benefits. "What was it in the beginning that was right for you?" "If it's different now, what is different?" "Does it affect certain perceptions of yourself or others?" "What about how you interact with others when using?" "What about your emotional experience when using?" "Is there a change in the way you experience any of your five senses?"

The questions can be exhaustive but don't necessarily need to be. Typically, once a person owns the reality that there is or has been some benefit to using a substance, a bit more comprehensive and forthcoming dialogue begins about this topic.

Note carefully the exact words used to describe benefits. You will be referencing those benefits as this procedure unfolds. The client's own words will tap into whatever meaning the client has ascribed to them. Interpretation and variation of the client's own words only complicate the procedure more than is necessary.

Some people will be very straightforward and specific while responding to questions about benefits. They may already have perfect clarity about why they are using a substance. They also haven't been ready or willing previously to give up those benefits.

The reality some people will face sober isn't very pretty. These people may be quite hopeless about anything in their lives changing for the better. There may be little hope or desire to cut free of what little relief they cherish. This kind of person will likely scoff at the preposterous possibility of getting certain needs met without embracing what has worked for them up to now.

As practitioners we best approach clients with no expectation of the specific ways change may occur. The person we work with may not change a thing, in spite of our best efforts. That person will learn something, however, and likely won't forget it.

Step Three - A pivotal question

Once you have information about substance use benefits, you are ready to create a little psychic jolt. Ask the question "If there were a way for you to get the best parts of the substance use experience without using X or any other substance, would this be desirable for you?"

Expect laughter or a sneer or a rolling of the eyes. Of course it's a silly question. And of course you'll get a yes response most of the time. Some will demand more information before answering, as if it were some kind of contest or trick question.

This then leads to a discussion about learning - physiological learning in particular. Examples of single exposure learning in humans and lower animals provide useful illustration of how the body absorbs information. The immune system learns about invading organisms quickly and records the information in order to recognize and conquer the invader upon its next approach. An infant puts a hairpin in an electrical socket only once to learn about electrical shock and this learning doesn't require cognitive analysis or feedback. When a dog eats something that makes it sick, it usually doesn't indulge in that food again.

Much evidence is now available about how information substances, as functional ligands, carry information between various organ systems and the central nervous system. Various peptides also link with the endocrine system and have an influence on neurotransmitters. Information about emotional experience is being transmitted between the immune system and the central nervous system. Many loops of information transmission keep the unconscious mind aware of multiple layers of experience and learning. Communication is always happening within the living body. Learning takes place at a physiological level on up to cognitive and psychological levels. Learning from new experience is recorded, often at a number of different levels simultaneously.

The psychobiological system probably learned all it needed to know about a particular substance after the first use. The learning about emotional, physiological, perceptual, cognitive and sensory experience is all there in a personal bio-library. The unconscious mind has access to what is stored in that bio-library. The desired information about substance use can be retrieved and employed.

Step Four -
Informing client about access to inner learning

Hopefully, you have captured your client's attention by this time. Many become curious about how desirable experience might be summoned. Skepticism is usually running high. Some will assume hypnosis must be involved because the unconscious was mentioned. Some will express great trepidation at the thought of hypnosis.

There is much mythology in western cultures about losing control under the spell of hypnosis. You can take a few minutes to dismiss fallacies and to offer accurate information about therapeutic hypnosis as a vehicle to gain much more personal control by accessing so many valuable inner resources. The hypnotic subject is in charge of his or her trance and able to go deeply into the inner experience or come out of trance at will.

It may be simpler to say that no hypnotic induction is necessary for this procedure. Inform the client that there exists a simple way to open a channel of communication with the unconscious without using any hypnotic induction. There exists a simple way to access information from the psychobiological "library" within. Suggest how the unconscious is communicating through the body all the time. Watching two people have a conversation we see heads nodding in agreement or shaking with disapproval. Hands are often gesturing as particular postures speak volumes. Most of that body language is automatic and involuntary. It is unconscious expression.

We can employ body language in a very intentional manner by allowing the unconscious to lift one finger for a "yes" response and a different finger for a "no" response. The responses are out of the realm of conscious volition as the client remains in full control and fully alert. This becomes a very pleasant way for a person to witness the autonomous functioning of the unconscious mind and get proof of the presence of an intelligent force within them- a force whose only purpose is to help.

Step Five - Communicating with the unconscious

Invite your client to set up a signaling system with the unconscious as described in Chapter Five. Help your client develop "yes" and "no" ideomotor finger signals. As you begin to see even very slight vibrations in a finger or coupling of fingers, share your observations with the client. You might say, "I'm seeing some small movements already…. Small movements that may add up to a larger movement as that signaling finger lifts up very easily."

Some people won't feel anything as a finger moves. These people may need to position hands in a way that allows them to view even slight finger movements in order to establish credibility. Other people won't care so much whether a finger movement is felt.

Step Six - The substance-state

After establishing ideomotor finger signals, suggest that the unconscious can now respond to questions through the finger movement. A preface to step six that affirms client control asks the question "Is it alright to continue communicating using the finger signals?" Hopefully you will get a yes response and be able to continue.

If you get a no response, ask, "Is this not the right time to continue with this process?" It may be entirely possible that the client is not quite ready to proceed.

Better to stop now and continue with full readiness at another time.

As you are clear about unconscious sanctions to continue, ask, " Is it alright now to call up the very best of the X experience as you described it earlier?" Reflect back the words used by the client to describe the benefits. If you get a "yes" response, acknowledge the response with something like "Yes, so that can now happen. Let yourself enjoy."

Step Seven - The benefit state tool

Then ask your client "Please touch the thumb and index (pointer, first) finger on the ___(right or left, whichever is the non-signaling hand) hand together and let those fingers continue touching for a little while." This sets up a physical trigger or anchor for the benefit state experience. If your client doesn't put those fingers together readily, announce that the fingers on that hand can be moved with conscious volition, full conscious control. The client doesn't need to wait for the unconscious to do it. Some people, after experiencing involuntary finger movements, assume all subsequent finger movements will be without conscious involvement.

The physical anchor can be any sort of distinct body positioning. I like the finger touch because it is simple and inconspicuous. One person had become a bit cataleptic as the benefit-state began to develop and her two fingers did not come together as requested. She was sitting with the left leg over the right leg at the time and this became her benefit state anchor.

Once an anchor is positioned or in place for utilization, say "As the unconscious recognizes this process of delivering the very best of using X experience is fully engaged, when its really happening, that yes finger can lift up as a signal at that time". After getting an affirmative finger signal, ask your client to tell you about the experience in words. Remind the client how only the best parts of the substance experience were requested, so it likely will be a little different than actually using X.

Some will just say "Its weird". If nothing more descriptive is uttered, ask about the client experience relative to each specific benefit previously described. Get some sense of the client experience.

As the client affirms an acceptable experience, ask "Will you now be able to access this same or even more intense experience of the best parts using X whenever you desire it by simply touching those two fingers together on that (right or left) hand (or whatever physical anchor was established) and expressing your intention inward?" You might add "Is it alright to have this kind of signaling system so you can access the best of X whenever you need it without using the actual substance?"

Acknowledge a "yes" response to the above question with favor and review the steps for soliciting the *benefit state tool* (BST), i.e. "You now have an X tool you can use any time, any place. All that's necessary to use this tool is to put those two fingers together on that (right or left) hand and say something like 'I'd like the best of X now please' and let things happen." The intention or request can be expressed aloud or silently.

This is an appropriate time to ask the client is he or she would like to intensify the experience even more. If the client wants more intensity, have the client put that request inward as those two anchoring fingers are touching. This is a wonderful way for clients to recognize how much influence over experience is available to them.

A negative response to the BST question

A "no" response to the BST question means there is something else to investigate. Guilt, shame or fear may need to be resolved before anything else can happen. Perhaps the language used to define the BST is too closely associated with negative consequences, memory or triggers to substance use. Perhaps some as yet undefined internal adjustment needs to precede the establishment of a BST. Are there changes in the client's environment needing attention first? There are numerous possibilities. Questioning at a conscious or unconscious level to understand more is appropriate.

Adopting a *harm reduction* (Denning, 2000) orientation is important at this juncture. There may be other concerns or dynamics needing attention before sobriety is possible. Plotting the course to sobriety often requires navigating through a hierarchy of obstacles. The obstacles define pieces of a client's inner reality and need to be handled with care. A gentle investigation clarifies client priorities and orchestrates how treatment proceeds.

An intravenous methamphetamine user with whom I worked refused this BST step. Her guilt prevented her from receiving something "good" and she wasn't able to continue with the procedure at this crossroad. She also only used this drug with others who were using at the same time. After she took steps to release the guilt she was able to access the best of that methamphetamine experience.

Naming the BST

For most previously involved in substance abuse treatment, finding the right name for the BST is critical. Calling up the best of the heroin experience or the alcohol experience is not going to be favorably embraced because there is often a deeply embedded all or nothing indoctrination regarding substance use. Sometimes talking and thinking about the best of a substance experience is too triggering. Why not let the client create a name for the BST that has characteristic meaning and relevance?

A man whose substance use history was quite extensive called his BST "Mr. Clean". A woman who had struggled with alcohol named her BST the "butterfly effect". It really doesn't matter what the tool is called. Ideomotor responses just need to confirm that a request for ___(name of BST) combined with the physical signal will summon the best elements of the substance use experience.

Once a person desiring a different name for the BST has selected a desirable name, go through the same questioning you did earlier in this step. Make sure the client is experiencing the benefit-state and have the client enact the physical signal for the BST. Ask "Will you be able to access this same experience, the very best aspects of using X as you have defined them, simply by putting those two fingers together on that (right or left) hand and expressing your desire for____ (name chosen for BST) inward?" An affirmative response to this question represents a contract from the unconscious mind for a functional BST.

Describing the BST

The language initially used to elicit a definition of the substance benefits may have, from the start, triggered alarms at the good/bad, all or nothing intersection developed from prior treatment indoctrination or the accumulation of negative consequences related to substance use. Be especially sensitive to this possibility when working with anyone who has had prior substance abuse treatment.

A more naturalistic reframe of the optional BST goes like this: "Given that the needs you've addressed by using

X are very valid needs, and given that you naturally wanted a way to address those needs, and given how the natural resources you have within you to address those needs were not fully available to you until now, and given your desire for a beneficial change, is it not in your best interest to develop a very natural, healthy way of addressing those needs at this time?"

> The "is it not?" form of inquisition typically presents enough ambiguity to the unconscious to provoke an examining pause, no matter what the content of the question. This question does not specifically say what will address these needs. The question doesn't reference the BST but there is an implication hanging in the air.
>
> A "yes" response could be "Yes, it is not in my best interest to develop this signaling system" or "Yes, it is not in my best interest to address those needs." A "yes" could also mean, "Yes, it is in my best interest to develop this signaling system… or address those needs." A "no" response poses the same ambiguity.

Whatever response is given to the "Is it not" question, respond with "Is it alright now to develop a signaling system which really uses the natural resources in you to experience the benefits only the X use gave in the past? … A better way to address those honest needs." A "yes" response invites "Will you be able to access this same or more intense experience of the benefits you described to me earlier without using any substance, simply by touching those two fingers together on that (right or left) hand and expressing your intention for the benefit-state inward?" Or "Will you now be able to access this same or more intense experience of those benefits whenever you desire it, simply be putting those two fingers together as they are now and expressing your intention inward?"

An affirmative signal is a contract for the BST to become operational. A "no" signal leads to more questions.

Other Adjustments

What about some adjustment, internal or external, required to facilitate the development of the BST? Asking the following questions will narrow the field of possibilities:

Q1. "Is there some adjustment needing to take place within you before you can develop a signaling system to call up the best of X without actually using any X?"

Q2. A "yes" response to Q1 can be politely met with "Given your intention to stop using the real drug and your ability to call up the best parts of using X, will that adjustment now take place for your benefit?"

- ♦ Ask for a specific finger to lift up when the adjustment is complete if you received a "yes" response to Q2 and then proceed with developing the BST.

♦ A "no" response to Q2 generates questions aimed at identifying temporal possibilities or type of adjustment needing to happen. For instance: "Will this adjustment happen within the next 24 hours, 48 hours, week, etc.?" Or "Does this adjustment involve emotional change?" Or "Does this adjustment involve a particular belief? Learning?"

Q3. A "no" response to Q1 inspires "Is there some adjustment needing to take place outside of you before developing a signaling system to call up the best of X without actually using any X?" If you get an affirmative response, ask "What needs to happen for you (client name)? Please tell me in words." Be patient awaiting a response.

More than once a client has spoken of a need to empty the bladder in response to this question. Other times a client will speak to a need to break off contact with a supplier and commit to that separation before securing an unconscious endorsement of the BST.

Sometimes further questioning indicates the adjustment needed is of an emotional nature. Emotional adjustments are the focus of Chapter Eight.

Step Eight - Goodbye letter

The client is now presented with the behavioral task of writing a goodbye letter to whatever substance was being used. This step is a way to ratify and ground the change process. Writing a letter engages tactile senses and formalizes thought into written word. It requires focus and attention. It also provides documentation and evidence to support intention. Constructing this letter is a formal ritual that marks a point in time when intention and resources converge to make a desirable change happen.

This proposal to write a letter provides an opportunity to discuss and position important aspects of the change process. The good bye letter acknowledges the end of a relationship, just as a Dear John or Dear Jane letter would. Ending a relationship, even when it's the best thing to do, always involves adjustments. Normalizing possible or likely adjustments aloud helps define a process the client will get through. All the elements of grief may be present. Habits, expectations, behavior patterns, perceptions, emotions and attitude are all subject to adjustment.

Encourage your client to be as comprehensive as possible with the farewell formality. Presenting an outline of letter topics is helpful for some. Consider sharing the following themes with a client:

- The purpose the relationship served, in the beginning and more recently.

- The benefits of the relationship.

- The problems and detriments of the relationship.

- The associations (people, places, events, activities, times of day, circumstances etc.) you have with the relationship.

- The influences the relationship has had on you.

- How you <u>feel</u> about letting go of this relationship.

- What you have learned from your experience in the relationship.

- What you will gain and what you will be giving up as you end this relationship.

- Be sure you have said <u>everything</u> you need to say before signing off.

Grief often plays a significant role in the transition to sobriety. Discussing the elements of grief, as well as the process of moving through grief, helps to normalize change dynamics. Most clients will easily recall past experiences of grief and relate to stages of denial, anger, depression, negotiation and acceptance. Some will need to grieve the loss of a perceived identity romantically interwoven with substance use. Some will discover they never grieved the loss of a loved one, either because of the emotional insulation provided by substance use or because the substance provided an experiential link to the loved one which denied their loss.

The goodbye letter sets the stage for a discourse about

grief and invites the client's excursion through the varied terrain of grief. Applying the *Goldfinger* approach described in Chapter Eight can gently accelerate the grief process.

Not everyone will write the goodbye letter. Some will fear being evaluated on their writing skills or the content of their message. I tell clients I don't need to read the letter. I encourage clients to say everything they want and need to say by way of ending the relationship they have had with that substance. The writing may take two or three sittings before it feels complete.

At times, this eighth step of the US procedure is equally well suited as the first step. When the intention to change substance use habits is first expressed, I will sometimes suggest writing a goodbye letter before doing anything else. A willingness to write the letter coupled with a completion of the process says much about sincere intention and motivation. The client's letter writing process is well worth exploring and validating. I acknowledge the letter as something quite significant and encourage the client to keep it in a safe place. Some have framed their letters. Others have positioned letters where they had previously kept their "stash".

This termination formality doesn't work for the person intending to "cut down" on substance use without abstaining altogether. Developing a BST is still a good option for this circumstance, as it provides another choice. A playful variation on the goodbye letter, if this type of behavioral ratification is deemed appropriate, might be a "I need a little time to myself" letter or a "downsizing format" letter.

Withdrawal options

Medical oversight, when possible, is always encouraged. There exists sufficient evidence of medical complications from rapid drug or alcohol withdrawal to warrant concern. Delirium tremens, among other things, can be life threatening. Heavy substance abuse is obviously also life threatening.

If your client is under the care of a physician, secure a release of information to talk with the physician before proceeding with treatment. Explain to the physician what you intend to do and coordinate a follow up visit to the doctor very soon after the US intervention. If the client displays no adverse withdrawal symptoms upon examination by the medical doctor, then treatment continues as planned.

Another option involves coordinating a withdrawal schedule with client and doctor. There are many variations to this option which largely depend upon the substance in question and the orientation of the medical professional. The client, after successfully developing a BST, may be instructed to alternate actual substance use with application of the BST. A ratio shift with increasing BST usage is mapped out.

This same approach applies to the use of ancillary

prescription medication, such as methadone or buprenorphine in place of the target substance. A schedule, coordinated with the prescribing medical provider, for alternating use of the prescription drug with the BST is set up. Withdrawal symptoms will signal the client to use either the medication or the BST.

Even though I have witnessed people gently withdraw from seriously addictive substances using the BST without any pharmaceutical intervention, I am well aware that most physicians and other professionals working with substance abuse clientele see a need for medical and/or pharmaceutical intervention. Given the history of substance abuse treatment to date and evidence of medical complications, this makes perfect sense.

Another option for the withdrawal phase of treatment involves frequency of visits. Whether a client is on a gradual withdrawal schedule or not, there may be benefit to scheduling daily or every other day visits to your office. The purpose of the visits is a way to track progress and any symptoms possibly needing medical attention. The visits also vigorously encourage the use of the BST, always asking the client to use it in the office. The client is encouraged to explore adjusting the "dose" of the BST, making it more or less intense via internal request. This is often quite empowering for the client. These frequent visits are only for the short term until sobriety is stabilized and withdrawal symptoms dissipate. The next steps of treatment focus on maintaining sobriety and recovering from any relapse, as discussed in Chapter Nine.

♦

We have reviewed the conditions necessary to begin applying the *Utilization Sobriety* method and the eight initial steps of *Utilization Sobriety* treatment, with various contingencies. We considered various options for withdrawal from a substance. The next chapter will explore a few possibilities for fine tuning the benefit state tool.

Chapter Seven

Fine Tuning the Benefit State Tool

The first qualities of our nature, like the bloom of fruits, can be preserved only by the most delicate handling.
Thoreau

There are many possible embellishments to the benefit state tool. The possibilities are only limited by your own or your client's imagination. To illustrate what is possible, I will share only a few of the useful high performance features that clients have added to their benefit state tools.

Adjusting Dosage

A week after developing an alcohol BST, Tim acknowledged how his alcohol tool was helping him refrain from drinking. He added that he wasn't feeling too good. I asked Tim to review for me exactly how he applies his alcohol tool and exactly what he imagines throughout the experience.

Tim had been limiting his BST experience to beer. In pre-treatment reality Tim typically chased beer with whiskey until reaching the desired destination of *Total Oblivion*. This destination was desirable because there was no pain and no guilt about not feeling pain. It seemed Tim had been rather automatically weaning himself off a very specific experience (oblivion). The needs normally addressed by alcohol were only partially quelled and seemed to be demanding more attention.

I complimented Tim on paying attention to his intuitive guideposts. A gentle reminder about the BST being only about the *best parts* of the alcohol experience seemed to calm Tim. Another reminder of how the BST provides a healthy, caring, appropriate experience for self, caused Tim to say "Even though I say I think I can control it before I start drinking, the whiskey is powerful and takes over. I was afraid of going there and losing control."

We explored how Tim really was having only the beer experience when he used the BST. I assured him that the alcohol tool was there to help him address the same needs actual drinking had addressed in the past. He had not only an effective escape option, if he needed or desired it, but a healthy "channel changer". I suggested Tim request whatever level of intensity best addresses the level of his needs at any given time.

Tim didn't realize he could exercise that much control over the BST. He practiced taking the BST to its extreme extension safely in our session. He then recognized a greater depth of the BST and the control he had. He didn't lose control of anything but his tension. He didn't lose good judgment or analytic perceptual facility. He was quite alert and responsive. He was able to feel good and focus on things other than his emotional pain.

He had a choice about using what he needs when he needs it in a very healthy manner. This allowed Tim, in subsequent sessions, to address and resolve some of the troubling emotional themes he harbored.

Adjusting the intensity of experience with the BST is always a worthwhile experience in session. Some clients will be embarrassed initially about their experience and be willing to talk about it only after shedding whatever shame was contaminating it. Others will candidly disclose "This works. This is what I want." It is always best to validate whatever experience the client is having. The client may be in the middle of some change or preparing for a change or concluding an adjustment or just recognizing change. As it all happens in a receptive, expectant and welcoming environment, various changes, including new perceptions, are anchored.

Even incremental change in the client is evidence of client control of, or influence on, present experience. There is no harm in reflecting this observation to the client and ratifying a hopefully empowering client perception.

This is but one complementary improvisation that amplifies the facility of a client's *benefit state tool*.

Regulating Duration

Celia sought treatment for an addiction to percocet, an opioid pain relief medication. She developed a percocet tool and reported delight in experiencing its effectiveness. Celia did, under a pretense of humor, wonder why the tool didn't work longer. Discussing this matter, Celia did realize the initial jolt she experienced from her previous dose of real percocet was of a similar duration to her BST.

I asked Celia if she had a kitchen timer at home. She replied affirmatively and said "Wouldn't it be nice to have one of those on this percocet tool." I asked Celia to close her eyes and "imagine what the right kind of timer looks like for your percocet tool. Is it an alarm clock? Or is it more like a kitchen timer? Why not use that timer on your percocet tool? Depending upon your circumstances, maybe setting it for 30, 45 or 60 minutes or…"

Celia found wonderful compliance with her timer and had no more complaints about her BST. Setting a timer for many different purposes often secures a predictability and expectation about limits and range of experience. Knowing the alarm clock is set, for example, when going to bed defines a specific amount of time for sleep.

This second client innovation involving the duration of the BST may reflect the maintenance of a desired physiological state. Or it may be nothing more than the result of giving permission for a desired experience. Permission is about authority and oversight. It sanctions authorized change.

Regardless of how or why this particular high

performance addition works, fine-tuning with a timer provides a perception of much greater control- a blessing to those with obsessive-compulsive proclivities.

Exploring the functional details of a client's BST paves a path to myriad manner of customizing and optimizing the tool. This then reinforces a client perceptual shift that affirms an internal locus of control. A pleasant, healthy, self-affirming way to take charge is a reality.

Some fine-tuning can certainly be done as the BST is being developed. As the client discloses his or her benefit state experience, adjustments in experience and the parameters of experience can be made. After a very satisfactory experience is reported, the BST can be defined and established.

Sometimes emotional adjustments need to be addressed before significant fine-tuning is possible. This will be explored next.

Chapter Eight

Resolving Emotional Obstacles to BST Formation

There is nothing like returning to a place that remains unchanged to find the ways in which you yourself have altered.
                    Nelson Mandela

There are many different approaches therapists employ in treatment to help a client heal psychological wounds and resolve emotions from the past. A relatively non-invasive method for unloading the emotional past will be described here because it employs ideomotor questioning. This allows the practitioner to be consistent with the US treatment methodology.

I find the emotions most often obstructing the development of the BST are guilt and shame. Fear presents itself as an obstacle occasionally. Fear and guilt often seem to function as gatekeepers, safeguarding the release of other contained emotions and halting particular changes until the gatekeepers themselves are disarmed.

Until questioning the unconscious about the specific nature of the refusal to develop the BST, you can only guess about psychodynamic roadblocks. Given that emotional perspective and attunement are diverted or circumvented with chronic or habitual substance use, addressing emotional themes may become a higher priority for the unconscious mind than sobriety. Many people begin using various substances as a way to cope with their emotional distress.

As a general guideline, help a client to resolve only the emotions posing as obstacles to development of the BST. Other emotions can be addressed after developing the BST. The BST, for some, will assist greatly in the processing of other emotions. If a person started using a substance as a way of coping with intense emotions, then the BST will provide some insulation needed to confront these emotions in a tolerable fashion.

Ideomotor questioning provides great facility with which to navigate the emotional terrain at this intersection. The generic exploration of emotional themes is done in a very non-invasive manner. Resolution of emotional states may happen very quickly. Consider how working with the unconscious in this way allows access to what I call dream time. Dream time is the expansive orientation to time and space we find in our dream and trance states. Ten minutes of clock time may be sufficient for a one-month vacation in dream time. Ideomotor questioning engages the unconscious mind and allows much to happen quickly, relative to clock time.

After receiving a "no" reply to the request for the BST, you may get a verbal explanation about the refusal that will guide your next step. In the absence of a verbal account, questions like the following can be put to the unconscious:

- "Is there some other adjustment needed before you can develop a signaling system for the best parts of the X experience without using any real X?"

- If you receive a "yes" response to the above question, ask, "Will that adjustment take place now in whatever way is best for you?" Or continue with the next question. If a "yes" signal indicates the adjustment can take place, encourage it and ask for a specific finger signal when the adjustment is complete. Then develop the BST.

- "Is there some emotion that needs to be released before you can develop a signaling system for the best of the X experience?" If a "yes" response, then let further questioning narrow the field of emotions. Start with guilt or shame as a safe bet. An approach I find very useful in resolving past emotion using ideomotor questioning is called the *Goldfinger* method (Walsh, 1997). The following is an elaboration on this method.

The Goldfinger Method

This procedure intends to reduce the adverse influence of past emotion on present experience. The emotional resolution portion of this procedure is a variation on methods developed by Cheek and LeCron (1968). Following emotional resolution is a ratification sequence intended to ground emotional adjustments in thought and behavior.

Before pursuing an emotion, inform your client about the possibility of experiencing alterations in thought, feeling, imagery, sensation or nothing at all as the unconscious responds in helpful ways. The unconscious is questioned in a concise and respectful manner about specific emotions. All questions are geared for a "yes" or "no" response as the predetermined finger signals provide answers and confirm changes. Remind the client intermittently that the unconscious has all the time it needs to develop the most appropriate response.

During this questioning phase the client may define a resolution hierarchy for emotions. Emotional pain, for instance, may need to be resolved before anger can be released. Specific information, themes or associations may become apparent at this juncture. Some form of abreaction may take place with noticeable movement and physiological alterations like flushing, tearing, breathing pattern shift or something else. Abreaction is most often silent.

Some level of trance may occur during questioning as you maintain focus and sparsely validate all client responses. The resolution interval before ideomotor confirmation of each emotional shift may be less than a minute or as long as 20 minutes. Sometimes a longer interval is needed to prepare for resolution. During a subsequent session (following the session in which resolution took place) consider posing the ideomotor question "Is there any other guilt (or other emotion) from the past that has not been resolved at this time?" This is an attempt to be thorough and possibly access any ego-states (Watkins, J., 1992) or internal parts not responsive to prior questioning and resolution.

The eight steps formally involved in the *Goldfinger* procedure are outlined in Box 3 and defined in subsequent text. Figure One is a questioning tree for identifying and resolving emotion.

Box 3.

Goldfinger Procedure

1. Develop rapport with client.

2. Develop ideomotor finger signals.

3. Establish comfort.

4. Question the unconscious about emotional content.

5. Ratify immediate affective experience.

6. Ratify cognition.

7. Ratify imagery with future orientation.

8. Ratify behavior.

The naming of emotions may need to be adapted to a client's unique perspective. For example, a young man whose presentation, in my estimation, clearly reflected anger and hostility said he wasn't angry. He confided having a lot of resentment. If he had anger, as he explained, something or somebody would have been hurt. This person appropriated specific language to various positions on the continuum of anger, based upon his behavior. Most of us do the same thing when considering the fear continuum. Fear may range from avoidance to nervousness to anxiety to panic and intense terror.

For most people the use of common emotional language with words like anger, fear, guilt, emotional pain or sadness will work fine. When in doubt or with evidence from a client's presentation, use more inclusive groupings of emotional terms. An inquiry about anger then becomes "Is there any anger or resentment or irritation or rage from the past that you continue to carry with you at this time?" An inquiry about emotional pain could become "Is there any emotional pain, sadness, hurt or heart break from the past that you continue to carry with you at this time?"

The following series of questions reflect this ideomotor questioning approach and represent variations on the questioning tree shown in Figure One.

Identification and resolution of emotion

A1. "Is there any guilt (shame, fear, anger, emotional pain or…) from the past you continue to carry with you?" A yes or no answer defines the field of emotions as yet unresolved. Once an emotion has been clearly identified, the client may or may not begin to talk about the context related to the emotional experience spontaneously. Proceed with the following after any client disclosures.

A2. "Since you have already been through all the experience of the past and you have whatever learning from experience can serve you well in the present, will that guilt (or other emotion) now be released and resolved in whatever way is truly best for you at this time?" Following a "yes" response, ask for a specific finger signal indicating completion of the resolution and freedom from that emotional load. Await the signal before proceeding.

B1. If you get a **"no" response to A2**, the request for emotional release, ask, "Is there some important information you need to understand very clearly to allow the release of this guilt (or other emotion)?"

> **B2**. Follow a **B1 "yes" response** with "Will that important information now come to conscious awareness so you can benefit from understanding it at this time?"

> **B3**. Follow a **B2 "yes"** with "As you have that

information in a way you can clearly understand it, that yes (or no) finger can lift up and you'll be able to talk about it, if you choose." Await that signal and whatever discourse may follow.

B4. A **"no" response to B2** prompts "Will that important information come to conscious awareness within the next twenty four hours (or two days, week etc.)?"

B5. You can sometimes shorten the process after a **B1 "yes"** by asking "Will that important information become very clear to you as the guilt (or other emotion) is resolved?" Following an affirmative response to this question, ask for a specific finger signal when the information is secured and the emotion is resolved.

B6. Follow a **B1 "no" response** with "Is there some other emotion that needs to be addressed first before guilt can be resolved?" A "yes" response brings you back to A1 to inquire about another emotion.

Socratic questioning guides this investigation of the emotional past. Each ideomotor response leads to another question. The above series of questions illustrates the process and certainly does not represent an exhaustive list.

Ratification

Emotional adjustments may extend to cognition, perception and behavior very consequentially and automatically following an emotional resolution. With no certainty that changes have extended in a comprehensive manner, the following measures to integrate emotional changes into thought, imagery and behavior do no harm and reinforce change. The following steps attempt to ground affective change in subsequent client experience under the guise of ratification.

Ratifying Immediate Experience

Various forms of ratification follow the release of whatever emotions are addressed. Ratifying the immediate resolution experience can provide a powerful grounding and affirmation of client reality. One form suggests to the client "perhaps the unconscious will provide additional confirming signals the conscious mind can appreciate, which reflect the changes taking place." As a resolution completion is signaled, consider a reflection like "That's right, free of that guilt (or other emotion). Maybe you feel that change in some way, at some level." Any acknowledgement of change happening helps ground and validate client experience.

Cognitive Ratification

This step seeks assurance that the cognitive process is

aligned with emotional change. After confirmation of an emotional resolution, inquiries designed to reinforce a boundary between previously limiting cognitive constructs and contemporary adaptive options can help. A shift like this can and does often occur automatically. The questioning approach illustrated below intends to confirm or prompt cognitive adjustments.

The following questions, or variations of these questions, are posed to a client after securing confirmation of an emotion being resolved. This step of ratification may be applied to a single emotion or collectively to a group of emotions.

C1. Solicit a specific ideomotor response (i.e. yes or no finger lifting) from the client as you ask "Since you are now free of that emotional burden of the past, is there a place in the past where all the thoughts, perceptions and learning no longer appropriate in the present can rest, out of the way of the present?"

C2. Or ask "Is there a place in history to put to rest all the thoughts, perceptions and learning that was somehow linked to the emotion that has been resolved?"

C3. Or ask "Now that the (emotion) has been resolved, will those thoughts, learning and perceptions previously linked to past (emotion) be positioned in the past where they will not interfere with present or future experience?"

C.4. Or if guilt was addressed, you might ask, "Given that you're now free of that guilt, will you offer yourself forgiveness at the deepest level possible?"

Resolving Emotional Obstacles

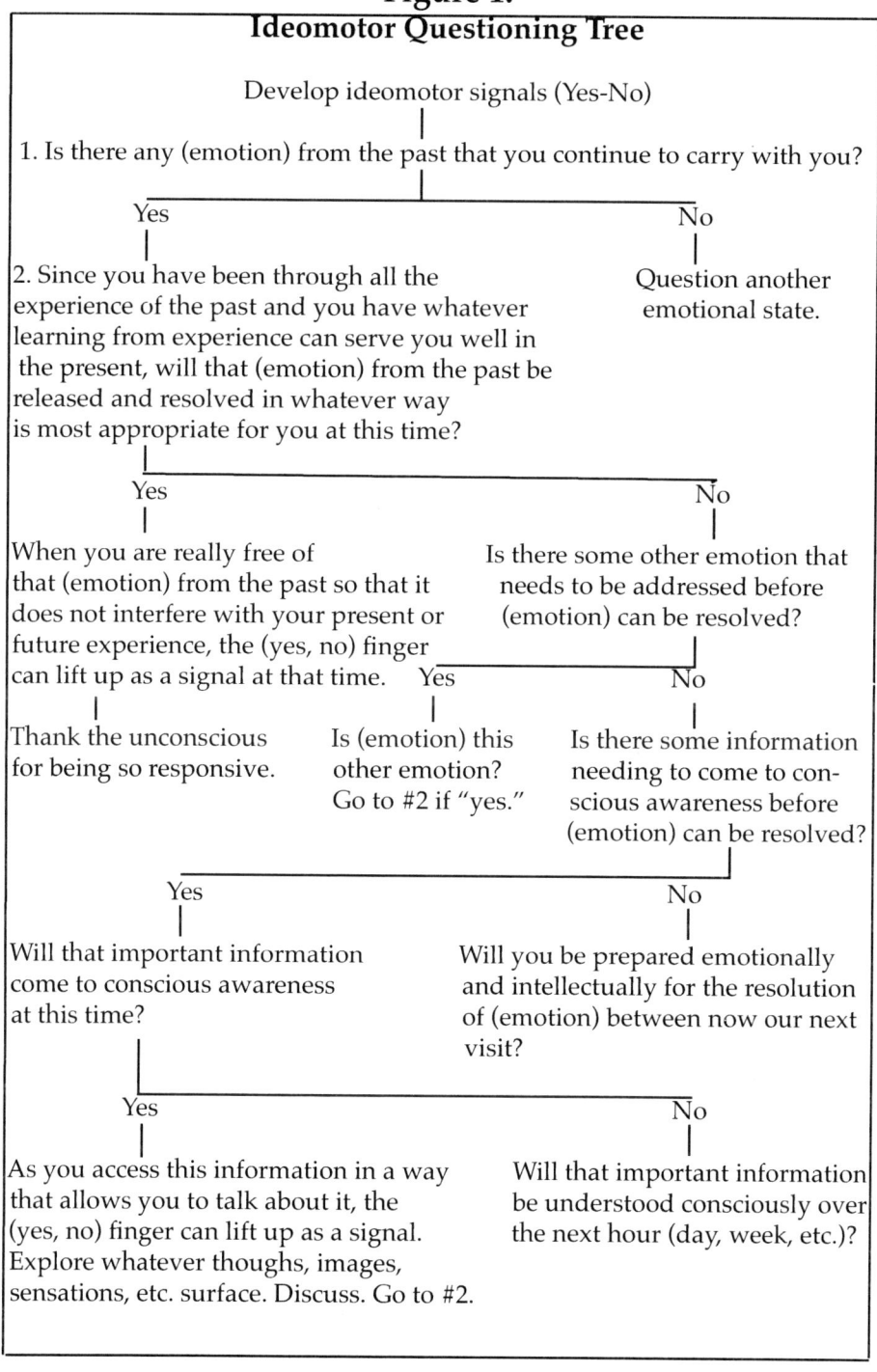

Figure 1.
Ideomotor Questioning Tree

> A **"yes" response to C1, C2, C3 or C4** prompts "So that adjustment can now happen. When that adjustment is complete, the "yes" finger can lift up as a signal at that time."

C5. A **"no" response to C1, C2, C3 or C4** invites "Given that you will still have an awareness of your past history after repositioning those thoughts, perceptions and learning no longer appropriate in the present, is there really any benefit to maintaining those things in the present?"

> A **"no" response to C5** initiates a repeat of a question similar to **C3**.

> A **"yes" response to C5** suggests the cognitive ratification be postponed and may prompt the client to discuss particular themes surfacing during ideomotor questioning.

C6. Or a **"no" response to C1, C2, C3 or C4** can cause you to ask, "Is there something important you need to understand very clearly before those adjustments can be made?" A "yes" response prompts a question like B2.

A **"no" response to C6** may indicate the presence of another layer of emotion not yet resolved. There may be deeply entrenched belief or learning not easily budged and requiring more therapeutic focus. Negative or positive responses to these questions guide subsequent questioning and inform a therapist about conditions possibly impeding therapeutic progress.

Imagery Ratification - future perspective

If ideomotor responses reflect cognitive alignment with the affective resolution, another temporal shift helps reinforce these gains. How can emotional relief endure without some degree of cognitive congruence and grounding in the external world? A future picture can serve as a behavioral compass at times. Developing a clear picture or sense of how desirable change is experienced in the future will impede anxiety significantly and also fuel hope. There are numerous ways to seed this experience. Consider how presenting the following speculations might guide client experience:

D1. After suggesting eye closure to a client, I imply "Perhaps a picture is already developing which informs you of just how your experience can be, now that you are free of so much from the past… recognizing how your thoughts, emotions, perceptions and behavior can be with the freedom you now have."

D2. Or I might suggest "This may be just the right time to let the unconscious develop a picture or sense of how your experience can be now that you are free of so much from the past. As you have that understanding very clearly, a "yes" finger can lift up as a signal at that time."

D3. Or I might ask, "Now that these important

adjustments have taken place, what is the first realistic step you see yourself taking to mark this occasion?" Allow plenty of time for the client to ruminate on this question. An answer to this question provides the raw material for the next step of behavioral ratification.

D4. Pulling the procedure back to the sobriety theme, I ask, "Now that these important adjustments have taken place, I wonder if a clearer picture develops of you having ended your relationship with X …perhaps a clearer sense of realizing an important change?"

Any of the above suggestions implies real change is happening and will be extended into the future. This implication, at the very least, seeds hope. Perhaps it also adds something new to the client's psychic landscape of the future.

Behavioral Ratification

This part of affect resolution is about what a client does and assumes the inevitability of client action. How will a client securely ground this emotional resolution? How will this change be acknowledged as a reality? What behavioral step or sequence will a client use to honor personal change?

The previous step of ratifying future imagery now needs to be enacted in some way. It is fairly common for fear to surface in a client while planning an enactment or just before taking the first steps of enactment. Fear may be experienced as nervousness, anxiety or panic. Fear may also come in a disguised form as it infiltrates thoughts in the form of procrastination and rationalization. In my experience fear almost always accompanies challenges to inner reality or incongruity between behavior and foundation beliefs and learning. Fear has a wonderful way of preserving the status quo. Informing a client about this dynamic and how quickly fear dissipates after actually taking that step associated with change is usually quite beneficial. I suggest the client consider taking fear along as a traveling companion with change, instead of letting it function as a braking system that inhibits change. When asked, many will be able to reflect upon the way fear colored successful changes of the past.

Within the context of *Utilization Sobriety* the behavioral ratification may be as simple as following through with treatment. If the next step of the US procedure is developing the benefit state tool, then this conveniently serves as a behavioral ratification. Other creative plans may surface in response to the questions of the previous section. Of most importance here is that the client develop a plan for doing something to acknowledge desirable change taking place and then follow through with the plan.

Some clients will devise specific rituals relevant and meaningful to them. One gentleman constructed an elaborate ship from a milk carton and loaded it with items representing what he was purging from his life. He set the ship adrift on a local river.

Elaboration

The full sequence of resolution and ratification usually takes place over a series of visits. As an attempt to reinforce prior gains, a session begins by asking the client to thoroughly review our previous work at an unconscious level and provide a finger signal when the review is complete.

The steps outlined here rarely happen sequentially with a single affective state in my practice. Most often two, three or four states are identified and resolved before the ratification series is fully explored. Double checking resolution in a later session by politely inquiring about the presence of "any other guilt (or other emotion)" indirectly appeals to any ego-state involved with that emotion and clarifies the appropriateness of further ratification.

The ratification process is central to the Goldfinger model. Although beneficial change may be realized in many clients without elaborating ratification procedures, some people are so entrenched in cognitive and behavioral patterns that affective alteration is imperceptible or only minimally noticed. For others familiar associational networks and environmental responses quickly veto unconscious adjustments. Client progress can be arrested easily without proper reinforcement. Taking much care to stabilize an affective shift is quite worthwhile.

Affective containment may develop as a result of

automatic unconscious forgetting (Laughlin, 1983) or, conscious attempts to bury undesirable emotion (suppression). Ideomotor questioning without inducing a deep trance facilitates search and adjustment potential at both conscious and unconscious levels simultaneously. Development of deeper trance states is then at the discretion of the unconscious and based on the distinctive needs of the individual.

Questioning affective themes, as opposed to content laden information, leaves the option of releasing or continuing to conceal past information to the unconscious. This avoids any unnecessary re-traumatization. The uncovering of historic artifacts is an option left completely to the unconscious.

The *Goldfinger* method can be a useful adjunct to other treatment processes. It is non-invasive, allowing the therapist to maintain a position of ignorance as a curious, concerned investigator. Goldfinger does not challenge client defenses, as obstacles are simply met with further inquiries. Ratification steps foster improved ego strength and autonomy by incorporating affect, cognition and behavior into the change process.

If, after resolving one emotion, there is still reluctance to establish the BST, inquire about other emotions needing to be released. There may be a full series of emotions ostensibly seeking resolution, but only one or two demanding resolution before the BST can be established.

The BST may function as insulation from accumulated emotion for many people. This is true, of course, when a client defines a substance benefit as "not feeling the (emotional) pain" or "a disconnect from my emotions" or "able to relax". This insulation will accommodate subsequent treatment dealing with past themes or current dynamics by allowing an individual to pace emotional experience as needed. I encourage clients to use the BST as much as needed to regulate their emotional experience in a tolerable manner.

Everyone moves through this kind of procedure in his/her own unique way. Some people feel the emotion as it wells up inside and then leaves. Some people see a stream of pictures as emotions are processed. Some people experience physical sensations during the release. Some people notice nothing at all as changes take place quietly at an unconscious level. It is a little different for everyone.

Since accumulation of past emotion speaks to a lifetime of experience, don't expect that everything will be cleared in one sitting. This could happen, but as the unconscious is invited to orchestrate whatever is best for the client at hand, emotion may be titrated out sequentially, requiring a number of passes.

♦

The *Goldfinger* procedure solicits emotional release with

ideomotor questioning and then attempts to fortify emotional resolution by ratifying thought, imagery and behavior. This particular way of negotiating emotional obstacles to the US treatment sequence incorporates the same operating modality as *Utilization Sobriety* and thus allows somewhat seamless movement between these two functions.

Chapter Nine

Sobriety Considerations

Curiosity is as much the parent of attention as attention is to memory.
Richard Whately

Motivation and Timing

Timing is important when considering the establishment of sobriety. What is the level of motivation for change in the person you're working with? Is this person just curious about what you have up your sleeve or does this person really want some change? What circumstances exist in this person's life, which either favor or contraindicate sobriety at this time?

If this is not deemed the right time to establish a *benefit state tool*, what changes are necessary to make things right? Is your client adequately aware of and willing to exercise choice as it applies to social circumstance, environmental incentives to use a substance and self-care?

Many have very part time or infrequent relationships with various substances. These people dabble in a substance or use it only circumstantially or on particular occasions or consider substance use experimental, explorative or recreational. Some view substance use as part of the past but don't entirely rule out present use. For many different reasons these people keep themselves from developing full time dependencies on a substance. Some of these folks are extraordinary exceptions to the rule as they sample very addictive drugs and resist the lure of continued use.

A common theme involves the person intending to only dabble in or sample a particular addictive substance who then falls under its spell. The "spell" certainly involves the biochemistry of the substance that creates a physiological dependence. Another aspect of the spell is about the perceptual shift it creates. The shift may affect memory as it transforms or obscures the past. Perception of present circumstances may be deluded, minimized or unrealistically exaggerated.

Consider a man who only views himself in a positive, responsive and accepting way when under the influence of marijuana. This is the only time his baseline anxiety is quieted. This is the only time his thoughts slow down enough to let him stay fully present, even if he thinks he is at other times. The marijuana gives him much facility to connect fully with his senses in the present tense. Some parts of inner reality are either uncovered or masked by the marijuana state. How will abstinence from pot smoking affect the quality of this man's life?

Consider the young woman, Nori (Chapter Five), who had an introduction to heroin while in the deepest grief about her mother's sudden death. Nori's mother was a guiding force in this young woman's life and in an instant she lost her compass. The only relief she found from her sorrow and anger was with a new chemical companion. Heroin, by her report, allowed her to function and deal with people. She was also aware of how the future that her mother had inspired was being stolen by heroin. Recognizing the trap wasn't enough to free her of its grip. Would this woman fare well without heroin if there were no other supports or coping strategy in place?

Consider a man who began drinking with his father at age thirteen. These were bonding experiences when dad offered guidelines about how to deal with women, definitions about real manhood, solutions for conflict and more. Drinking times with dad were historic markers and reference points. A foundation was still being constructed during these adolescent years. These were the corner stones of sexual identity and social relevance that carried over into adulthood.

Who is this man if he stops drinking? What terror wells up in him at the very thought of not drinking? How can he be a man without drinking? So much learning, perception, belief and behavior is wrapped up in the alcohol-state.

At one level, motivation to change is inspired, if not birthed, by the specific balance between benefit and detriment regarding a particular behavior or pattern. When the balance produces problems of a magnitude greater than the perceived benefits, it is time to, at the very least, consider change. The seed of motivation is planted and even sprouting! This is often the time when people make inquiries about professional help.

If the perceived benefits of an ongoing behavior far outweigh the trouble spots, motivation to change that behavior will likely be weak or non-existent.

Sometimes a learning-based fear provides motivation for change, even when the scale is tipped heavily in favor of benefits. Nori (Chapter Five) said heroin was the only thing that made life tolerable. It covered up her emotional and physical pain, allowed her to interact with people acceptably and felt good. She had prior learning, however, about the seductive trap door through which many never returned. She had witnessed other heroin-seduced lives trapped and spiraling downward. She knew she would never make anything better in her life if she continued with heroin. This gave her motivation to change. Fear about completely losing the future became a detriment that tipped the scale in favor of change.

Client motivation is probably the single most important indicator of treatment success with substance abuse treatment. If a person calls to get a treatment appointment, there is some degree of motivation. If a person shows up for treatment, a measurable level of motivation exists. Once a client is in your office, you'll be able to assess the particular dimensions and driving forces of motivation. If motivation seems too low initially, then amplifying motivation becomes the focus of treatment.

When motivation is perceived high and favorable to planned interventions, a different order of intervention begins. It is, I believe, always good to initially incorporate steps for the augmentation of motivation. Reinforcing and referencing motivating factors often is very appropriate.

When a person demonstrates little or no motivation for change, postponing an ostensibly remedial intervention is warranted. This becomes a time for you to be curious about why the client does not really want change. Is there a different goal, seemingly unrelated to substance abuse treatment, which holds the client's motivation? How is this person going to convince you change is even desirable? How has this person's passion been expressed in the past? Does this person's passion or desire for change ever get expressed? Is this person really wanting change but not versed in any appropriate expressive idiom?

Perhaps your assessment is accurate and there really is no motivation for changing the status quo. Perhaps the scale is heavily weighted in favor of maintaining substance use behavior. This, of course, supports taking a pause in treatment and reflecting your assessment to the client.

◆

Consider the stages of change model (Prochaska et al,

1994) as another perspective when motivation has not yet surfaced. The stages include:

1. <u>Precontemplation</u> represents a stage at which a person has little or no intention to change. This person usually has inadequate information with which to consider change.

2. <u>Contemplation</u> is a stage that finds a person recognizing the existence of a problem and thinking something should be done about it.

3. <u>Preparation</u> is a stage embracing intention to change and the establishment of behavioral criteria for that change.

4. <u>Action</u> is the stage at which behavioral change is happening and a person is attempting to follow through with a commitment to self.

5. <u>Maintenance</u> is the stage in which new learning and behavior is supported with coping strategies intended to sustain changes made.

6. <u>Termination</u> signifies the stabilization of change.

Efforts to seed motivation can be nicely tailored to the stage of change a client manifests. This option is particularly helpful with mandated clients. At stage one, the treatment provider supplies salient information to the client if it is deemed absent. Focused curiosity about a client's inner and outer reality then guide a therapist's questioning and reflection.

Milton Erickson brilliantly demonstrated tactics for inspiring or extending motivation (Erickson & Rossi, 1976, 1979) in the way he posed inquiries and shared his observations. Erickson suggested "Resistances constituting a part of the problem can be utilized by enhancing them and thereby permitting the patient to discover, under guidance, new ways of behavior favorable to recovery" (Erickson, in Rossi, 1980).

Some of the key elements Erickson applied are represented in the user-friendly treatment approach called *Motivational Interviewing* (Miller & Rollnick, 1991). *Motivational Interviewing* flows nicely through the stages of change. It intends to build the client's motivation to change and strengthen the client's commitment to change. The basic operating principles of *Motivational Interviewing* include:

♦ Expressing empathy.

♦ Developing discrepancy by emphasizing client awareness of detriments to substance use.

♦ Avoiding argumentation as client perspective is explored.

♦ Embracing any perceived resistance as client ambivalence is acknowledged and validated.

♦ Supporting self-efficacy.

The particular questions asked and the specific content reflected back to a client are fine tuned to the stage of change the client seems to be engaging. A person, for instance, at the precontemplation stage may be inclined to talk about emotional distress rather than substance use problems. There may be much motivation to feel better emotionally. Discussing emotional experience is a way to engage the treatment process, validate coping strategies, question contributions to emotional distress and plant motivational seeds for substance use dynamics.

◆

Curiosity is a lure that often becomes a powerful motivator. Why not bait a hook and see if the client bites? This is when I focus questioning only on the benefits of whatever substance is in question. I interrupt a person who wants to elaborate on the negative consequences of substance use, the trouble he or she has been in, the occupational and social detriments, the health problems, the financial cost and so on. Instead, I ask about the particular needs and wants the substance use addresses. How does it help? What does it help? When does it help? What kinds of circumstances does it help with most?

This line of questioning, which is embedded in the *Utilization Sobriety* approach and compatible with Motivational Interviewing, indirectly acknowledges the ambivalence common in most seeking substance abuse treatment and typically disrupts or creates an imbalance in a person's usual reality. When someone comes for substance abuse treatment, that person typically expects to be questioned about and even lectured on all the negative consequences of substance use. So expectations are disarmed and a little bit of curiosity might emerge.

I then continue with step 3 of the *Utilization Sobriety* procedure. The big bait comes with the step 4 question "If you could get the best aspects of using X that you described to me earlier without using X or any other substance, would this be desirable?" I follow this with "We can talk about this in more detail next time we meet, if you have any interest in discussing it."

The above usually stirs up some curiosity. Much of the time the curiosity becomes a powerful motivator. Sometimes little curiosity seems evident and this tactic just doesn't work.

◆

Motivation exists on a continuum and needs to be at a certain level before any kind of treatment intervention for substance use has a chance of working. What exactly moves motivation along that continuum? We've talked about detriments of substance use, benefits of substance use, curiosity, fear about the future and fear driven by learning and logic. There are also social, occupational and familial dynamics that affect motivation.

Another motivation factor influencing all of the above

is physiology. Motivation really has psychobiological drivers and is on a psychobiological continuum. Relatively recent discoveries in human biochemistry and gene expression provide more evidence for this motivation matrix.

On a macrodynamic level, we can go to state dependent learning, memory and behavior. Whenever a substance of choice is introduced to the body, a signature physiological state is established.

A particular state established by a foreign chemical substance not produced in the body typically influences concentrations of various neurotransmitters and peptides. Depending upon the duration of substance use, some substance states can alter cell structure. Based on supply and demand, cells may sometimes produce fewer receptor sites for particular molecules. These physiological changes can serve to reinforce drug cravings.

At a limbic level, some substance states may resonate well with survival needs. Consider post-traumatic stress situations where the energetic fight-flight-freeze response is quelled during substance use. Many survivors of trauma don't seek or get adequate treatment and find a semblance of peace through chemical means. This relief from endogenous stress becomes a powerful, deeply unconscious motivation to continue using the substance.

On a micro level we can examine how each substance

communicates with the body-mind. If we consider the central nervous system like the hard drive of a computer, the neuropeptides carrying information intercellularly, intracellularly and system-wide would be the software of the computer. Each substance we use, in addition to creating a particular psychobiological state, affects the normal flow of "software" communication in the body-mind. In a computer, we might get a message on the desktop screen saying "unexpected program error - shut down program and restart computer" or "could not find translator to open this file" or " program requires more memory than available". Just imagine what happens in our system when the normal flow of communication is altered biochemically. Each class of substance creates some kind of alteration in its own way.

Temporarily shutting down certain programs in the "computer" sometimes is important for those reacting to overwhelming circumstances. Variations on post-traumatic stress disorder (PTSD) represent this kind of situation. If certain "programs" don't shut down, the entire system could crash. There is, of course, the natural and adaptive symptomatic shut down experienced as dissociation and amnesia. When the natural system isn't sufficiently effective at re-routing particular "files," many suffering from PTSD will seek relief from some kind of substance. This accounts for the high percentage of trauma survivors in substance abuse treatment.

A lot has already been said about biochemical,

physiological and cellular communication as it relates to drug or alcohol use. I have outlined a little about the role of specific cellular receptor sites, the lock and key mechanism that provides a functional gate to limit and specify intercellular and intracellular communication. Molecular "impersonators" like those of the opiate configuration key into receptor sites normally intended for the body's own endorphins. We examined how unlocking certain receptor sites stimulates another level of communication that influences production and concentration of specific neurotransmitters. We know those neurotransmitters are very closely linked with motivational incentives, influencing thought, perception, emotion, behavior and the maintenance of substance use patterns. We glimpsed at how the introduction of substances with "fake identification", able to access receptor sites, significantly alters system wide communication.

How might this system wide change in communication and perception influence gene expression? We all inherit a particular complement of genes. Some genes represent a static condition, unchanged by environment or experience. We have blue eyes and brown hair and nothing is going to change that genetic expression. Other genes, however, only turn on or turn off in response to environmental, circumstantial or interpersonal experience. Many soft tissue disorders fit this category. Not all members of a family carrying cancer genes express cancer. For those who are genetically inclined, psychosis generally finds a starting "break" time and circumstance at which it becomes a reality.

If certain genes get turned on and turned off by what is biochemically communicated to them as a result of particular conditions, might communication errors or alterations have some effect on gene expression?

There are genes carried in family lines that indicate a propensity for alcoholism. Not everyone in a family like this becomes an alcoholic. The potential may be there but the alcoholic genes may never get turned on.

I don't want to spend too much time at the intersection of gene expression and substance use states because there is yet too little known about this and I thus resort to hypothesis. This is, however, another factor potentially influencing the motivation continuum.

◆

To come full circle, let's go back to *Utilization Sobriety*. This motivation discussion could be left as some unmanageable continuum. The good news is that you have a way of accessing multiple levels of motivation in the people you work with. From the first session you are approaching your client without judgment and full of curiosity about what is working with the substance. There is no shame induction. A relational context is established which may come as a surprise to the client. Surprise and novelty are very good things in this setting. One of three conditions suspected of being favorable to neurogenesis in the brain is novelty

(Rossi, 2002). The other two conditions include exercise (movement) and environmental enrichment (a favorable context or environment).

The first session establishes a new perceptual framework if curiosity is piqued sufficiently. Talking about the mastery of psychobiological learning is often empowering to many. The re-establishment of psychobiological choice is a big one. Framed in this way, the client realizes no choice is taken away with sobriety. The client is simply reclaiming a right to full choice. This also comes to many as a surprise.

Establishing a way of communicating directly with the unconscious is often a novelty as well. Pondering the possibilities associated with this new skill is empowering and really affirms autonomy. Developing ideomotor signals provides evidence of a non-conscious intelligence within which functions independent of conscious volition. This can easily create a new perspective.

The experience of calling up the best of the substance-state is more novelty and a potentially powerful influence on both physiological and psychological motivation for change simultaneously. The needs addressed by the substance are addressed without the substance. A change is felt and developed completely from within - a victory for self-regulation and autonomy.

These factors may have a favorable influence on

motivation.

Sobriety Maintenance - Relapse Recovery

After developing a satisfactory BST, I explain to clients that some degree of actual drug use after acquiring the BST is not uncommon. Some people recognize from the first session that they can really follow through with their decision to end the relationship with a substance and still get what they need. These folks do a quick, clean break and no longer have contact with that substance.

Others need more time to adjust to the change or to make adjustments in their social world. Some don't believe its real- it's too easy! Time may be needed to integrate a new reality.

The most important consideration is realizing there is a choice about using that substance. The BST will deliver the best of the substance without the ill effects. Changes in behavior, habit, social contacts, thought, perception and emotion can all accompany a real divorce - a divorce from anything or anybody.

Relapse happens more often than not for a vast number of reasons. I focus much more attention on relapse recovery than relapse prevention. Anticipating the possibility of relapse, without necessarily predicting it, normalizes this possibility and reinforces an awareness of choice. There is no benefit to inducing shame about relapse for most people. Many people end their relationship with a substance in the same manner they end a romantic relationship with a person. They may do things very gradually, dragging out some of the not so subtle nuances. Some will need to experience one last good bye. Others will need to test this change and their ability to refrain or regroup after using a substance.

Many people need much beyond a painless detoxification or means of addressing the needs previously met by substance use. The condition for which some are self-medicating may need to be addressed sequentially as they move toward sobriety. For others, self-defeating behaviors and personality dynamics demand alteration to sustain sobriety. Relapse triggers can be seen as iatrogenic, prompted by the external environment, or autogenic, prompted through some internal, endogenous dynamic.

Physiological adaptation has, I surmise, significant influence on the particular ways people end a relationship with substance and maintain distance from the substance. Scientific evidence mapping the mechanisms of self-reinforcing biochemical demand for a substance suggests that external sensory cues and even memories can alter neurotransmitter balance in the brain and produce drug seeking behavior (Adelman & Smith, 1999 p.22). The theory of *incentive sensitization* developed from this evidence suggests that the brain's mesolimbic dopaminergic system becomes progressively more sensitive to environmental stimuli that have been regularly linked with drug availability. This stimulus then elicits the same motivational response that the drug itself does. The environmental stimuli may in this case encompass any drug using association like a street name, a piece of music, a picture of a needle and much more.

One alcohol study (Langenbucher, Sulesund, Chung & Morgenstern, 1996, p547) poses "results consistent with self-efficacy theory, indicating that the most severely dependent subjects are those with the least confidence that they will be able to abstain from drinking under a variety of high-risk conditions." Various characterological and developmental themes, of course, may need to be addressed by treatment in some fashion for many to sustain sobriety.

Marlatt and Gordon (1985) explain the goal of relapse prevention is "to increase the client's awareness and choice concerning their behavior, to develop coping skills and self-control capacities, and to generally develop a greater sense of confidence, mastery, or self-efficacy in their lives". Treatment strategies maintaining a categorically pathological focus can reinforce or induce shame and, for some, a sense of victimization. This is contrary to stabilizing or augmenting the esteem, self-directedness and sense of empowerment complementary to maintaining sobriety.

Many common approaches to maintaining sobriety have great merit when tailored to the individual. "Triggers" or incentives to use a substance, for instance, lose some power when openly discussed in treatment. Triggers lose even more control when confronted by their host in a functional manner. Some clients benefit tremendously by developing assertive skills specifically rehearsed to manage triggers. Changing at least some social contacts or travel patterns is often the result of confronting triggers. Reviewing or **rehearsing trigger situation strategies**, especially when incorporating visual elements, is shamelessly supportive and affirming of choice as it develops a new picture. Confrontations may also take the form of self-talk and thought stopping without any strong visual component.

A support group may be what is needed for some to reinforce their gains. **Attending support group meetings** *of any kind* provides some new social contact with whom to test new behaviors or even a new reality. A support group can function as a reflection back to a client, simply validating that a change is taking place.

A support group is also an opportunity to compare relative positions on that track of time. How do my life and my experience compare with these other people? How differently or similarly are they dealing with their circumstances and choices? The possibility of forming new, positive relationships is yet another potential benefit.

Affect and Sobriety

The emotional and cognitive themes resulting from or driving substance use are important pieces that need to be dealt with as part of the self - relations contract for sobriety. In some cases the development of the BST was contingent on an agreement with the unconscious to address emotional burdens as the next step in treatment.

The *Goldfinger* approach to dealing with the emotional past, as discussed in Chapter Seven, is a nice companion to *Utilization Sobriety*. Employing unconscious resources allows much to happen in a relatively short amount of calendar and clock time. Sometimes emotional cargo is a powerful endogenous trigger.

The client has options about using the BST to insulate emotional experience until the time feels right to address affect. The client has options about securing unconscious help to resolve past emotional baggage in a non-invasive manner. The *Goldfinger* theme may need to be interspersed with other treatment activities, as tolerated by the client.

I always encourage clients to use the benefit state tool often and for whatever reason. Each session typically begins with a suggestion that the client use their BST as a nice way to get started. I remind them that the BST is a healthy way to manage stress, tension or anxiety. If the BST functions to insulate emotion and they need that insulation at any time, then using the BST is very appropriate. Specific emotional work can be designated for the treatment session.

Memory Functions

Triggers related to the emotional past can involve multiple layers of memory function. Memory functions serve both the US goal and the potential pitfalls of relapse. This relates to some fundamental principles that guide my thinking about the functional mechanics of *Utilization Sobriety*. The central nervous system (CNS) and the immune system learn and have memory (Solomon, 1990; Martin & Goodnon, 2000). The phenomenon of state-dependent memory, learning and behavior (Rossi, 1986 & 1993, Lynch et al, 1984) reflects a biochemical, systemic form of memory.

Memory interacts with and influences perceptual fields which in turn generate emotional response. Emotional response involves physiological change at some level (Pert, 1997; Frey, DeSota-Johnson, Hoffman & McCall, 1981). Anxiety, for example, illustrates how a perception of a future event interacts with an unpleasant memory and stimulates fear, which triggers the endocrine system to release epinephrine. Another example is sexual arousal resulting from the remembrance of a stimulating experience or picture. Allergic reaction demonstrates memory in the immune system. The physical body, recording the experience of five tangible senses with their affective associations and outcome judgments, remembers much.

A good portion of body memory is, of course, dedicated to survival. A preverbal infant learns functional avoidance after touching a hot burner once. A food causing illness is avoided thereafter. Tears begin to flow as a particular piece of music evokes a past emotional experience even before the narrative memory surfaces. All these things reference the interconnectedness of memory, emotion, cognition, physiology and behavior.

Memory's role in *Utilization Sobriety* is, of course, quite significant and goes well beyond an individual's historic recall. Memory can be processed, recorded and retrieved in different ways, depending on experiential circumstances, biological state, affective positioning and developmental stage of life (Brown et al, 1998). Pillemer and White (1989) present much evidence supporting what they call a behavioral memory system. Brown et al (1998) refers to this same system as "implicit memory" and suggests it is the mechanism by which traumatic memory is stored. This mechanism encodes memory for somatic experience, images, emotions, and behaviors and is conceptualized to be the primary memory system in the first years of life. Following the acquisition of language, Pillemer and White (1989) contend a second, narrative, personal memory system evolves parallel to the behavioral system. They call the second system "the socially accessible memory system".

When memory seems to be implicit or state-bound (Overton, 1972 & 1973; Rossi, 1993; Brown et al, 1998) in a biochemical matrix, it may or may not eventually come to narrative form. Ideomotor questioning is one way to access implicit memory (Brown et al, 1998; Cheek, 1994). Cheek (1994) suggests ideomotor questioning is a way to communicate at a physiological level, bypassing cognition altogether. I believe the experience of putting any mood or mind altering substance into the body produces a peculiar physiological state, binds at least some information to the state and goes far beyond what can be explained through cognitive means by the altered individual. If the substance-state overlaps, intersects or incorporates a particular emotional state, ideomotor questioning provides a means of negotiating beneficial adjustments.

Requesting the desirable aspects of a substance-state via ideomotor questioning likely accesses both the behavioral and socially accessible memory systems (Pillemer & White, 1989). Constructing a new perspective and context for the substance experience may catalyze other changes in cognition and physiology.

◆

Twelve Step Peace

Is *Utilization Sobriety* compatible with twelve step programs (Alcoholics Anonymous, 1939, 1976)? How does *Utilization Sobriety* mesh with twelve step programs? These questions are quite relevant to both treatment providers and those participating in twelve step recovery programs. Yes, a good deal of compatibility does exist between US and the twelve step model.

Twelve step programs originally began as support groups for recovering alcoholics. Treatment programs and support groups for many kinds of addiction now employ a twelve step format. The steps, as originally presented, are:

1. We admitted we were powerless over alcohol- that our lives had become unmanageable.
2. Come to believe that a Power greater than ourselves could restore us to sanity.
3. Made a decision to turn our will and our lives over to the care of God as we understood Him.
4. Made a searching and fearless moral inventory of ourselves.
5. Admitted to God, to ourselves, and to another human being the exact nature of our wrongs.
6. Were entirely ready to have God remove all these defects of character.
7. Humbly asked Him to remove our shortcomings.
8. Made a list of all the persons we had harmed, and became willing to make amends to them all.
9. Made direct amends to such persons wherever possible, except when to do so would injure them or others.
10. Continued to take personal inventory and when we were wrong promptly admitted it.
11. Sought through prayer and meditation to improve our conscious contract with God as we understood Him, praying only for knowledge of His will for us and the power to carry that out.
12. Having had a spiritual awakening as the result of these steps, we tried to carry this message to alcoholics, and to practice these principles in all our affairs.

For those following the twelve step protocol, steps four and ten focus on moral and personal inventory. Does a thorough inventory not encompass the whole person- body, mind and spirit? Is the functioning of that whole person not a part of the inventory? Are the physiological, psychological and spiritual resources of this whole person not a part of an honest assessment? How can a moral inventory not include the powerful psychobiological forces that influence moral action and thought?

The answers to these questions may seem quite evident because so much information is now available about the interconnectedness of the human system. US helps the twelve stepper do a more comprehensive inventory by acknowledging and employing inner resources as valuable aspects of self. Employing these resources may help an individual move through subsequent program steps.

When an alcoholic person develops an alcohol *benefit state tool*, there is no conflict with steps one, two or three. A person with a BST may still be powerless over alcohol, while having a means of naturally satisfying needs that alcohol previously quelled. This person is thus able to circumvent alcohol use with more facility.

For anyone believing in a God or some Higher Power, faith plays a significant role. Can this believer determine with absolute certainty that some intangible high order Force or spiritual presence is not playing a part in the development of a BST? Can this believer say with absolute certainty that the unconscious mind is not a convenient vehicle for spirit communication? If positive change is really happening as a result of seeking professional help and securing sobriety enhancing tools, might a God force be contributing to this development?

I believe *Utilization Sobriety* is remarkably compatible with the twelve step model as it solicits natural resources from the realm of the non-conscious. US can, however, meet resistance from fundamentalist twelve steppers who believe prolonged suffering is a necessary component of recovery.

The treatment provider's appropriate adjustment of language used during the US treatment typically softens client objections. This involves framing the procedure as a way of reclaiming natural resources, some of which only became evident after developing a dependence on a substance. Posing a few of the questions asked in this section will help resolve perceived discrepancies for some.

•

In this chapter we looked at factors influencing motivation and its role with intervention timing and treatment success. An overview of some strategies for maintaining sobriety included support group attendance, rehearsing trigger situation strategies, managing affect and frequent use of the BST. We examined memory's pivotal function in both the *Utilization Sobriety* method and as a potential trigger of substance use. A look at how US is compatible with the twelve step model concludes this discussion of sobriety considerations.

Sobriety Considerations

Epilogue

The manner of speaking is full as important as the matter, as more people have ears to be tickled than understandings to judge.
Philip D. S. Chesterfield

I hope this text has inspired some curiosity and recruited enough skepticism to guide your exploration, application and elaboration of this method. The guiding principles of this work, as outlined in Chapters Two, Three and Six, welcome improvisation and elaboration. The variations presented here on particular elements of the US procedure represent common peculiarities I encounter with clients. Many more variations exist which invite utilization and creative adaptation.

Utilization Sobriety grew out of me from the seeds others had planted. The "plant" continues to grow and change. It provides a comfortable means for me to address client concerns while engaging more of the client than just the discourse. And even the discourse between the person seeking help and the treatment provider, when approached in this way, is non-punitive and laced with curiosity. The delicate incorporation of a strengths perspective can foster hope and optimism.

Utilization Sobriety is certainly not a fix-all and may not be the right fit for some people. *Utilization Sobriety* is not a complete treatment. It is a piece of treatment that facilitates sobriety quickly and responds to whatever needs a particular substance addressed. For some, this piece of treatment may be the last or only piece needed to establish a desirable change. Others will require emotional or perceptual adjustments before they can implement a benefit state tool. For this kind of requirement, the *Goldfinger* approach is quite helpful.

The body-mind communication employed by *Goldfinger* allows for a smooth transition to and from *Utilization Sobriety*. Themes involving affect and emotion can be addressed as needed during the US process. Once sobriety is established, problematic emotional relics of the past invite attention. Timing is important at this intersection. Some people benefit greatly by confronting a triggering emotional past soon after sobriety is established. Others need more time to adjust to or apply their *benefit state tool*. Some need to titrate out emotional baggage sparsely or intermittently.

Utilization Sobriety offers a shameless, painless, self-empowering option that restores choice robbed by an addictive substance. The BST provides a means to address needs served by the actual substance use. As with any therapeutic endeavor, the tools provided in treatment may or may not be employed by the client. Ongoing treatment is often necessary for a time to reinforce choice options, identify and prepare for trigger situations, resolve precipitating emotional themes and cognition, reinforce frequent use of the BST and more. A highly motivated person may succeed with minimal intervention.

Epilogue

This model for substance abuse treatment simply utilizes what already exists in the person seeking help. Treatment employs psychobiological process and learning, enculturated themes about substance use, and idiosyncratic response to needs. *Utilization Sobriety* provides a quick and painless avenue for withdrawal from a substance while honoring adaptive strategies for living, surviving, coping and healing. The goal in developing the BST is both for relapse prevention and the bridging of prior coping strategies with new perspective. Using the BST is about developing a new habit and recognizing choices involving an inner locus of control. Exercising choice then becomes an important focus of therapeutic communications as the treatment goal is achieved or refined.

Writing about the evolution of *Utilization Sobriety* and body-mind communication allowed me to infer a theory of how a person achieves a relatively painless withdrawal from substance and how the BST functions. Since this method has not yet undergone the rigors of scientific analysis, I can only hypothesize an explanation.

Unconscious access to the biochemical basis of state-dependent memory, learning and behavior may allow for the activation of specific psychobiological components of that experience. This re-creation of desirable experience likely alters concentrations of information peptides that influence perceptual fields involved in sensation, emotion or cognition. Contracting with the unconscious to allow conscious access to the desirable state allows the formation of the BST.

How much control can one exert on biochemistry and physiology without using various substances? Anecdotal reports and empirical evidence cited by Weil (1995), Siegel (1988), Benson (1996) and Simonton (1978) tout the great influence that thought, perception and emotion have on physiology and health. The process of employing the perceptual elements of a client's past learning related to substance use may indeed elicit a particular physiological shift. A physiological shift may generate emotional, perceptual and even behavioral changes. Although I don't know what is happening at a physiological level with clients when they call up the best of their substance experience, their testimonials reflect an experiential shift that is often objectively observable.

Utilization Sobriety, like making a phone call, is a fairly simple procedure to execute. Information transduction in the body-mind system, like the telephone system, is quite complex. In the same way a telephone line can access tremendous amounts of information, so an open channel to the land of the unconscious allows the access of body-mind learning. This open channel provides a body-mind link to sobriety potentials.

This book represents what pieces of the puzzle I have put together thus far. I have seen enough positive change in the people I work with to warrant sharing this information with a broader audience. More steps need to be taken, however. Research has not been done

Epilogue

yet to track what is happening at a physiological and neurological level when people apply what they learn from this method. I look forward to the possibility that future scientific inquiry may shed light on what is really happening at the neuro-physiological level throughout the US process.

Thank you dear reader for considering this treatment option. Thank you for doubting and wondering as you navigated this text. I hope you find this a useful addition to your toolbox.

References

Ader, R.; Felten, D. L.; & Cohen, N. (Eds.) (1991). *Psychoneuroimmunology*, second edition. San Diego: Academic Press, Inc..

Adelman, G. & Smith, B. H. (1999). *Elsevier's Encyclopedia of Neuroscience*, second edition. Amsterdam: Elsevier, Vol. I.

Alasuutari, P. (1992). *Desire and Craving: a Cultural Theory of Alcoholism*. New York: State University of New York Press.

Alcoholics Anonymous World Services, Inc. (1939, 1955, 1976). *Alcoholics Anonymous*. New York, A.A. World Services, Inc.

Aminoff, M. J. & Daroff, R. B. (Eds.) (2003). *Encyclopedia of Neurological Sciences*, Amsterdam: Academic Press, Vol. I.

Bandler,R. & Grinder, J. (1981). *Trance-Formations*. Moab, Utah: real People Press.

Ibid (1979). *Frogs into Princes*, Moab, Utah: Real People Press.

Bandura, A. (1977). Self-Efficacy: Toward a Unifying Theory of Behavioral Change. *Psychological*

Review. 84: 191-215.

Barber, J. (1996). *Hypnosis and Suggestion in the Treatment of Pain.* New York, W.W. Norton.

Bateson, G. (1971). The Cybernetics of Self: a Theory of Alcoholism. Psychiatry. 34: 1-18. Reprinted in *Steps to an Ecology of Mind.* New York, Fireside.

Ibid (1972). *Steps to an Ecology of Mind.* New York: Ballantine.

Beck, A. T. (1976). *Cognitive Therapy and the Emotional Disorders.* New York: Penguin Books.

Benson, H. (1996). *Timeless Healing: The Power and Biology of Belief.* New York: Fireside.

Berne, E. (1964). *Games People Play.* New York: Ballantine Books.

Blalock, J. E. & Smith, E. M. (1985). A Complete Regulatory Loop between the Immune System and Neuroendocrine Systems. *Federation Proceedings, Federation of American Societies for Experimental Biology,* 44, PP 108-111.

Blalock, J. E.; Bost, K. I.; & Smith, E. M. (1985). Neuroendocrine peptide hormones and their receptors in the immune system. Production, processing and action. *Journal of Neuroimmunology,* 10. PP. 31-40. November, Vol. 29 (11): 2053-2062.

Blane, H. T. (1968). *The Personality of the Alcoholic: Guises of Dependency.* New York: Harper & Row

Bormann, N.M. & Overton, D.A. (1993). Morphine as a conditioned stimulus in a conditioned emotional response paradigm. *Psychopharmacology.* 112: pp 277-284.

Brown, D.; Scheflin, A.W. & Hammond, D.C. (1998). *Memory, Trauma, Treatment and the Law.* New York: W. W. Norton.

. Campbell, A.D.; Kohl, R.R., & McBride, W.J. (1996). Serotonin-3 receptor and ethanol-stimulated somatodentritic dopamine release. *Alcohol,* Vol. 13 (6): 569-574

Carter, R. (1999). *Mapping the Mind.* London: University of California Press.

Cheek, D. B. (1994). *Hypnosis: The Application of Ideomotor Techniques.* Needham Heights, Massachusetts: Allyn & Bacon.

Cheek, D.B. & Le Cron, L.M. (1968). *Clinical Hypnotherapy.* New York: Grin & Stratton, pp. 86-88.

Choi, I.Y., Allan, A.M. & Cunningham, L.A. (2005). Moderate fetal alcohol exposure impairs the neurogenic response to an enriched emvironment in adult mice. alcohol effects on the fetus, brain and other organ systems. *Alcoholism: Clinical and Experimental Research,*

November, Vol. 29 (11):

Colvin, R. (1995). *Prescription Drug Abuse: The Hidden Epidemic*. Omaha, Nebraska: Adictus Books, Inc.

Condiotte, M. M. & Lichtenstein, E. (1981). Self-efficacy and relapse in Smoking cessation programs.

Colvin, R. (1995). *Prescription Drug Abuse: The Hidden Epidemic*. Omaha, Nebraska: Adictus Books, Inc.

Condiotte, M. M. & Lichtenstein, E. (1981). Self-efficacy and relapse in Smoking cessation programs. *Journal of Consulting and Clinical Psychology.* 49, pp. 648-658.

Crenshaw, T. L. & Goldberg, J. P. (1996). *Sexual Pharmacology: Drugs that Affect Sexual Functioning*. New York: W.W. Norton.

Crews, F.T. & Nixon, K. (2003). Alcohol, neural stem cells and adult neurogenesis. *Alcohol Research and Health,* Vol. 27 (2): 197-204.

Denning, P. (2000). *Practicing harm reduction therapy*. New York: Guilford Press.

deShazer, S. (1988). *Clues: Investigating solutions in brief therapy*. New York: W.W. Norton.

DiChiara, G.E. Acquas & Tanda, D. (1996). Ethanol as a neurochemical surrogate of conventional reinforcers: the dopamine-opioid link. *Alcohol*, Vol. 13 (1): 13-17.

Edgette, J. H. & J. S. (1995). *The Handbook of Hypnotic Phenomena in Psychotherapy*. New York: Brunner/Mazel.

Edwards, G. (1966). Hypnosis in the treatment of alcohol addiction: controlled trial, with analysis of factors affecting outcome. *Quarterly Journal of Studies on Alcohol*. Vol 27, 221-241.

Ellis, A. (1971). *Growth Through Reason: Verbatim Cases in Rational-Emotive Psychotherapy*. Palo Alto: Science and Behavioral Books.

Ellis, A.; McInerney, J. F.; Giuseppe, R. D.; & Yeager, R. J. (1988). *Rational-Emotive Therapy with Alcoholics and Substance Abusers*. New York, Pergamon Press.

Erickson, M.H. (1992). *Creative Choice in Hypnosis*. Rossi, E.L. & Ryan, M.O. (Eds.) New York: Irvington Publishers.

Erickson, M.H.; Rossi, E.L. & Rossi, S.I. (1976). *Hypnotic Realities*. New York: Irvington Publishers, Inc.

Erickson, M.H. & Rossi, E.L. (1979). *Hypnotherapy*, New York: Halsted Press.

Essman, W. B. (1983). *Clinical Pharmacology*

of Learning and Memory. New York: S. P. Medical & Scientific Books.

Evens, K & Sullivan, J. M. (1990). *Dual Diagnosis: Counseling the Mentally Ill Substance Abuser*. New York, Guilford Press.

Floyd, A. S.; Monahan, S. C.; Finney, J. W.; & Morley, J. A. (1996). Alcoholism treatment outcome studies, 1980-1992: The nature of the research. *Addictive Behaviors*, Vol. 21, no. 4: pp 413-428.

Foreman, J. C. & Johansen, T. (Eds.) (1996). *Textbook of Receptor Pharmacology*. New York: CRC Press.

Fox, V. (1993). *Addiction, Change and Choice: The New View of Alcoholism*. Tuscon, Arizona: Sharp Press.

Frey, W. H.; DeSota-Johnson, D.; Hoffman, C. &McCall, J. T. (1981). Effect of stimulus on the chemical composition of tears. *American Journal of Ophthalmology*, 92(4), pp. 559-567.

Frost, R. (2002). *Applied Kinesiology: A Training Manual and Reference Book of Basic Principles and Practices*. Berkeley, CA: North Atlantic Books.

Fryer, J.D. & Lukas, R.J. (1999). Antidepressants non-competitively inhibit nicotinic acetylcholine receptor function. *Journal of Neurochemistry*. March 72(3): 1117.

Galizio, M. & Maisto, S. A. (Eds.) (1985). *Determinants of Substance Abuse: Biological, Psychological and Environmental Factors.* New York: Plenum Press.

Gallant, D. M. (1987). *Alcoholism: A Guide to Diagnosis, Intervention and Treatment.* New York: W. W. Norton.

Gentile, D. A. & Walsh, D. A. (2002). A normative study of family media habits. *Applied Developmental Psychology,* 23, January: 157-178.

Gilligan, S. (1997). *The Courage to Love: Principles and. Practices of Self-Relations Psychotherapy.* New York: W.W. Norton & Co.

Goldstein, A. & Hilgard, E. R. (1975). Failure of opiate antagonist naxolone to modify hypnotic analgesia. *Proc. Nat. Acad. Sci.* USA, 72: pp. 2041-2043.

Goodlet, C.R., Horn, K.H. & Zhou, F.C. (2005). Alcohol teratogenesis: mechanism of damage and strategies for intervention. *Experimental Biology and Medicine,* 230: 394-406.

Grevert, P. & Goldstein, A. (1978). Endorphins: naloxone fails to alter experimental pain or mood in humans. *Science,* 199: pp1093-1095.

Graybiel, A. (1999). The brain is not the same after chronic cocaine: network-level changes in basal ganglia circuits. In, Cocaine and a Changing Brain- *Meeting*

Summary (Oct. 1970). N.I.D.A., National Institutes of Health publication no. 99-4382.

Groff, S. (1985). *Beyond the Brain.* Albany: State University of New York Press.

Hall, F.S.; Li, X.F.; Sora, I.; Xu, F.; Caron, M.; Lesch, K.P.; Murphy, K.L. & Uhl, G.R. (2002). Cocaine mechanisms: enhanced cocaine, fluoxetine and nisoxetine place preferences following monoamine transporter deletions. *Neuroscience.* 115(1): 153-61.

Hartland, J. (1965). The value of "ego-strengthening" procedures prior to direct symptom removal under hypnosis. *American Journal of Clinical Hypnosis,* 8: 89-93.

Inaba, D. S.; Cohen, W. E. & Holstein, M. E. (1997). *Uppers, Downers and All Arounders: Physical and Mental Effects of Psychoactive Drugs.* Ashland, OR: CNS Publications.

Ibid (2004) Fifth edition.

Jellineck, E. M. (1960). *The Disease Concept of Alcoholism.* New Haven: College and University Press.

Jung, C. G. (1933). *Modern Man in Search of a Soul.* New York: Harcourt, Brace & World, Inc.

Jung, C.G. (1959). *The Archetypes and the Collective Unconscious.* New York: Princeton, Bollingen. p. 234

Kandall, S. R. (1996) *Substance and Shadow: Women and Addiction in the United States*. Cambridge, Ma.: Harvard University Press.

Klimek, V.; Schenck, J.; Han, H.; Stockmeier, C. & Ordway, G. (2002). Dopaminergic abnormalities in amygdaloid nuclei in major depression: a postmortem study. *Biological Psychiatry*, Oct 1; 52(7): 740

Knight, R. P. (1937). *The dynamics and treatment of chronic alcohol addiction*. Bulletin of the Menninger Clinic, 1: pp233-250.

Kreek, M. (1998). Neurobiologic correlates of the addictions: findings from basic and treatment research. *In Drug Addiction Research and the Health of Women. National Institute on Drug Abuse, N.I.H. publication no. 98-4290*.

Lader, M.(Ed.) (1988). *The Psychopharmacology of Addiction*. Oxford; Oxford University Press.

Laing, R. D. (1972). *The Politics of the Family and Other Essays*. New York: Vintage Books.

Langenbucher, J.; Sulesund, D.; Chung, T. & Morgenstern, J. (1996). Illness severity and self-efficacy as course predictors of DSM IV alcohol dependence in a multisite clinical sample. *Addictive Behaviors*, Vol. 21, no. 5: pp. 543-553.

Laughlin, H.P. (1983). *The Ego and Its Defenses.* New Jersey: Jason Aronson, Inc.

Lynch, G., McGaugh, J. & Weingerger, M. (Eds.) (1984). *Neurobiology of Learning and Memory.* New York: Guilford Press.

Madras, B. (1999). Cocaine targets in primate brain: liberation from prosaic views. In, *Cocaine and a Changing Brain- Meeting Summary (Oct. 1997). N.I.D.A., National Institutes of Health publication no.* 99-4382.

Maitra, R. & Reynolds, J.N. (1998). Modulation of GABA-A receptor function by neuroactive steroids: evidence for heterogeneity of steroid sensitivity of recombinant GABA-A receptor isoforms. *Canadian Journal of Physiological Pharmacology.* 76(9): pp 909-920.

Mann, P. (1985). *Marijuana Alert.* New York, McGraw-Hill Book Co.

Markianos, M.; Moussas, G.; Lykouras, L. & Hatzimanolis, J. (2000). Dopamine receptor responsivity in alcohol patients before and after detoxification. In *Drug and Alcohol Dependence,* 57: 261-265.

Marlatt, A. G. & Gordon, J. R. (1985). *Relapse Prevention.* New York: Guilford Press.

Martin, S. & Goodnon, C. (2000). Memory needs no reminders. *Nature,* Vol. 407, Oct.: 576-577.

Martin-Ruiz, C.M.; Court, J.A. & Molnar, E. (1999). Alpha 4 but not alpha 3 or alpha 7 nicotinic acetylcholine receptor subunits are lost from the temporal cortex in Alzheimer's disease. *Journal of Neurochemistry*. 73: 1635-1640.

Maslow, A. H. (1970). *Motivation and Personality*. New York: Harper & Row.

McCord, W. & McCord, W. (1960). *Origins of Alcoholism*. Stanford: Stanford University Press.

McClelland, D. C.; Davis, W.; Kalin, R. & Wanner, E. (1972). *The Drinking Man: Alcohol and Human Motivation*. New York: The Free Press.

McNeal, S. & Frederick, C. (1993). Inner strength and other techniques for ego strengthening. *American Journal of Clinical Hypnosis*, 4: 250-256.

Menninger, K. (1938). *Man Against Himself*. New York: Harcourt, Brace.

Miller, S. D. & Berg, I. K. (1995). *The Miracle Method: A Radically New Approach to Problem Drinking*. New York: W.W. Norton.

Miller, W.R. & Rollnick, S. (1991). *Motivational interviewing: Preparing people to change addictive behaviors*. New York: Guilford Press.

Nakkan, Craig (1996). *The Addictive Personality*.

Center City, MN: Hazelden.

National Institute on Drug Abuse (NIDA) (1996). Methamphetamine Research: Like methamphetamine, "ecstasy may cause long-term brain damage. Mathias, R. *NIDA Notes.* Volume 11, November/December.

National Institute on Drug Abuse (NIDA) (2000). Principles of Drug Addiction Research: A Research-Based Guide. *National Institutes of Health publication* no. 00-4180.

Nash, M. R. (2001). The truth and hype of hypnosis. *Scientific American*, July, 46-55.

Nixon, K. (2006). Alcohol and adult neurogenesis: Roles in neurodegeneration and recovery in chronic alcoholism. *Hippocampus,* Vol. 16 (3): 287-295.

Nixon, K. & Crews, F.T. (2004). Tempotarally specific burst in cell proliferation increases hippocanpal neurogenesis in protracted abstinence from alcohol. *The Journal of Neuroscience,* October 27, Vol. 24 (43): 9714-9722.

O'Doherty, F. (1991). Is drug use a response to stress? *Drug and Alcohol Depend.*, 29: 97-106.

Orman, David J., (1991). Reframing an addiction via hypnotherapy: a case presentation. *American Journal of Clinical Hypnosis.* April 33(4): 263-271.

Ornstein, R. & Swencionis, C. (1990). *The Healing Brain: a Scientific Reader.* New York: Guilford Press.

Overton, D.A. (1971). State-dependent of "dissociated" learning produced with pentobarbital. In: Harvey, J.A. (Ed.) *Behavioral Analysis of Drug Action: Research and Commentary.* Chicago; Scott, Foresman and Co.

Overton, D.A. (1972). State-dependent learning produced by alcohol and its relevance to alcoholism. In B. Kissen & H. Begleiter (Eds.), The Biology of Alcoholism. Vol. II, *Physiology and Behavior.* New York: Plenum, 193-217.

Overton, D.A. (1973). State-dependent learning produced by addicting drugs. In S. Fisher & A. Freedman (Eds.), *Opiate Addiction: Origins and Treatment.* Washington D.C.: Winston, pp. 61-75.

Overton, D.A. (1982). Memory retrieval failures produced by changes in drug states. In: Isaacson, R.L. & Spear, N.E. (Eds.), *Expression of Knowledge.* New York: Plenum Press.

Page, R. A. & Handley, G. W. (1993). The use of hypnosis in cocaine addiction. *American Journal of Clinical Hypnosis,* Oct. 36(2): 120-123.

Perls, F. (1976). *The Gestalt Approach and Eye Witness to Therapy.* New York: Bantam Books.

Pert, C. B. & Snyder, S. H. (1973). Opiate receptor: demonstration in nervous tissue. *Science* 179: 1011-1014.

Pert, C. B.; Ruff, M. R.; Weber, R. J. & Herkenham, M. (1985). Neuropeptides and their receptors: A psychosomatic network. *Journal of Immunology*, 135(2,Suppl.), 820-826.

Pert, C. B. (1986). The wisdom of the receptors: Neuropeptides, the emotions, and body-mind. *Advances*, 3(3): 8-16.

Pert, C. B. (1997) *Molecules of Emotion: The Science Behind Mind-Body Medicine*. New York: Touchstone.

Pillemer, D.B. & White, S.H. (1989). Childhood events recalled by children and adults. In H.W. Reese (Ed), *Advances in Childhood Development and Behavior* (Vol. 21, pp297-340). San Diego, Ca: Academic Press.

Prochaska, J., DiClemente, C. & Norcross, J. (1994). *Changing for good*. New York: Avon.

Randall, M.D. (2003). A new endothelial target for cannabinoids. *Molecular Pharmacology*, Vol. 63 (3). pp. 469-470.

Rosen, S. (1982). *My voice will go with you*. New York: Norton.

Rossi, E.L. (2002). *The psychobiology of gene expression*. New York: W.W. Norton & Company, Inc.

Rossi, E.L. (Ed.) (1980). *The Collected Papers of Milton H. Erickson, M.D.* Vol.IV. New York: Irvington.

Rossi, E.L. (Ed.) (1980, 1989). *The Collected Papers of Milton H. Erickson on Hypnosis.* Vol.II, Hypnotic alteration of sensory, perceptual and psychophysiological processes. New York: Irvington.

Rossi, E.L. (1986). *The Psychobiology of Mind-Body Healing.* New York: W.W. Norton & Company, Inc.

Ibid (1993). *The Psychobiology of Mind-Body Healing* (revised). New York: W.W. Norton & Company, Inc.

Rossi, E.L. & Cheek, D.B. (1988). *Mind Body Therapy: Ideodynamic Healing in Hypnosis.* New York: W.W. Norton & Co.

Schmitt, F. Chemical information processing in the brain: prospect from retrospect. In Iverson, L. & Goodman, E. (Eds.), *Fast and Slow Signaling in the Nervous System.* New York: Oxford University Press.

Schloss, P. & Williams, D.C. (1998). The serotonin transporter: a primary target for antidepressant drugs. *J. Psychopharmacology*, 12(2): 115-21.

Shaham, Y. (1993). Immobilization stress-induced oral opioid self-administration in rats: role of conditioning factors and the effects of stress on "relapse" to opioid drugs. *Psychopharmacology* 111: 477-485.

Shulz, D.E., Sosnik, R., Ego, V., Haidarliu, S. & Ahissar, E. (2000). A neuronal analogue of state-dependent learning. *Nature*, February, 2000, Vol. 403: pp 549-552.

Sideroff, S. & Jarvik, K. (1980). Conditioned responses to a videotape showing heroin related stimuli. *International Journal of Addictions*. 15: 529-536.

Siegel, B. (1988). *Love, Medicine and Miracles.* New York: Harper Trade.

Simonton, O. C. (1978). *Getting Well Again.* Los Angeles: Ballantine Books.

Snyder, S. (1986). *Drugs and the Brain.* New York: Scientific American Books.

Stanton, H.E. (1979). Increasing internal control through hypnotic ego-enhancement. *Australian Journal of Clinical and Experimental Hypnosis*, 7: 219-223.

Stanton, H.E. (1989). Ego-enhancement: a five step approach. *American Journal of Clinical Hypnosis*, 3: 193-198.

Stein, M. (Ed.) (1985). *Jungian Analysis.* Boston Shambhala.

Stoil, M.J. (1989). Problems in the evaluation of hypnosis in the treatment of alcoholism. *Journal of Substance Abuse Treatment* 6(1): 31-3

References

Trimpey, J. (1996). *Rational Recovery: The New Cure for Substance Addiction*. New York: Pocket Books. *Theory and Therapy*. New York: W.W. Norton.

Unterwald, E. M.; Horne-King, J. & Kreek, M.J. (1992). Chronic cocaine alters brain mu opioid receptors. *Brain Res*. 584: 314-318.

Vaillant, G. E. (1983). *The Natural History of Alcoholism: Causes, Patterns and Paths to Recovery*. Cambridge, MA: Harvard University Press.

Vandamme, T. H. (1986). Hypnosis as an adjunct to the treatment of a drug addict. *Australian Journal of Clinical and Experimental Hypnosis*. May 14(1) 41-48.

Van der Kolk, B. A.; Pitman, R. K.; Orr, S. P. & Greenberg, M. S. (1989). Endogenous opioids and post-traumatic stress. Paper presented at the *Annual Meeting of the American Psychiatric Association*, San Francisco.

Wadden, T. A. & Penrod, J. H. (1981). Hypnosis in the treatment of alcoholism: a review and appraisal. *American Journal of Clinical Hypnosis*, July 24(1), 41-47.

Walsh, B.J. (1997). Goldfinger: A framework for resolving affect using ideomotor questioning. *American Journal of Clinical Hypnosis*, 40(1): 349-359.

Walsh, B. J. (2003). Utilization Sobriety: brief, individualized substance abuse treatment employing ideomotor questioning. *American Journal of Clinical*

Hypnosis, 45(3): 217-224.

Walsh, B. J. (2003). Utilization Sobriety: brief, individualized substance abuse treatment employing ideomotor questioning. *American Journal of Clinical Hypnosis*, 45(3): 217-224.

Watkins, J.G. & Watkins, H. H. (1997). *Ego States: Theory and Therapy,* New York: W.W. Norton

Weil, A. (1995). *Spontaneous Healing.* New York: Ballantine Books.

Weiss, F. (1999). Cocaine dependence and withdrawal: neuroadaptive changes in brain reward and stress systems. In, *Cocaine and a Changing Brain- Meeting Summary (Oct. 1997). N.I.D.A., National Institutes of Health publication* no. 99-4382.

White, M. (1993). Deconstruction and Therapy. In Gilligan, S. & Price, R. *Therapeutic Conversations.* New York: W.W. Norton & Co.

White, M. & Epston, D. (1990). *Narrative Means to Therapeutic Ends.* New York: Norton.

Zhou, F.C., Sari, Y. & Powrozek, T.A. (2005). Fetal alcohol exposure reduces serotonin innervation and compromises development of the forebrain along the serotonergic pathway. *Alcoholism: Clinical & Experimental Research*, January, Vol. 29 (1): 141-149.

References

# Topic Index

abreaction xi
abstinence
    before US procedure 24, 25, 26, 27, 104, 165, xi, xii
acetylcholine 24, 25, 26, 27, 104, 165, xi, xii
action 24, 25, 26, 27, 104, 165, xi, xii
active imagination 24, 25, 26, 27, 104, 165, xi, xii
addiction 24, 25, 26, 27, 104, 165, xi, xii
affective themes 24, 25, 26, 27, 104, 165, xi, xii
alcoholics anonymous 24, 25, 26, 27, 104, 165, xi, xii
alcoholism
    disease model of
    causes of 24, 25, 26, 27, 104, 165, xi, xii
ambien 24, 25, 26, 27, 104, 165, xi, xii
ambivalence 24, 25, 26, 27, 104, 165, xi, xii
amnesia 24, 25, 26, 27, 104, 165, xi, xii
amphetamine 24, 25, 26, 27, 104, 165, xi, xii
amygdala 24, 25, 26, 27, 104, 165, xi, xii
anandamide
    receptor site
    function 24, 25, 26, 27, 104, 165, xi, xii
anchor
    benefit state
    substance state 24, 25, 26, 27, 104, 165, xi, xii
angel dust
    PCP 24, 25, 26, 27, 104, 165, xi, xii
anger 24, 25, 26, 27, 104, 165, xi, xii
antabuse 24, 25, 26, 27, 104, 165, xi, xii
antidepressant 24, 25, 26, 27, 104, 165, xi, xii
anxiety 24, 25, 26, 27, 104, 165, xi, xii
applied kinesiology 24, 25, 26, 27, 104, 165, xi, xii
argumentation 24, 25, 26, 27, 104, 165, xi, xii
associational networks 24, 25, 26, 27, 104, 165, xi, xii
autonomy 24, 25, 26, 27, 104, 165, xi, xii
barbituates 24, 25, 26, 27, 104, 165, xi, xii
behavioral compass 24, 25, 26, 27, 104, 165, xi, xii
behavioral memory 24, 25, 26, 27, 104, 163, 165, xi, xii
belief
    lens 24, 25, 26, 27, 104, 165, xi, xii
benefit state tool
    devlopment of
    timer
    adjusting intensity 24, 25, 26, 27, 104, 165, xi, xii
benzodiazapines 24, 25, 26, 27, 104, 165, xi, xii
bio-computer 24, 25, 26, 27, 104,

165, xi, xii
body language 24, 25, 26, 27, 104, 165, xi, xii
BST
    naming
    describing
    natualistic reframe 24, 25, 26, 27, 104, 165, xi, xii
buprenorphine 24, 25, 26, 27, 104, 165, xi, xii
butterfly effect 24, 25, 26, 27, 104, 165, xi, xii
cannabis 24, 25, 26, 27, 104, 165, xi, xii
catalepsy 24, 25, 26, 27, 104, 165, xi, xii
cataleptic 24, 25, 26, 27, 104, 165, xi, xii
channel changer 24, 25, 26, 27, 104, 165, xi, xii
chiropractor 24, 25, 26, 27, 104, 165, xi, xii
choice
    lens 24, 25, 26, 27, 104, 165, xi, xii
cocaine 24, 25, 26, 27, 104, 165, xi, xii
cognitive
    congruence therapy 24, 25, 26, 27, 104, 165, xi, xii
communication
    body-mind
    ambiguous
    unconscious 24, 25, 26, 27, 104, 165, xi, xii
    ideomotor 24, 25, 26, 27, 104, 165, xi, xii

consensus reality 24, 25, 26, 27, 104, 165, xi, xii
consequences
    negative 24, 25, 26, 27, 104, 165, xi, xii
contemplation 24, 25, 26, 27, 104, 165, xi, xii
continuum
    parallel
    dependence 24, 25, 26, 27, 104, 165, xi, xii
coping strategies 24, 25, 26, 27, 104, 165, xi, xii
cortisol 24, 25, 26, 27, 104, 165, xi, xii
craving
    approval
    substance 24, 25, 26, 27, 104, 165, xi, xii
curiosity 24, 25, 26, 27, 104, 165, xi, xii
deconstruction 24, 25, 26, 27, 104, 165, xi, xii
dependence
    continuum of 24, 25, 26, 27, 104, 165, xi, xii
depression 24, 25, 26, 27, 104, 165, xi, xii
disease
    model 24, 25, 26, 27, 104, 165, xi, xii
dissociation 24, 25, 26, 27, 104, 165, xi, xii
disulfiram 24, 25, 26, 27, 104, 165, xi, xii
dogma
    twelve step 24, 25, 26, 27, 104, 165, xi, xii

Index

dopamine
    receptor site
    function 24, 25, 26, 27, 104, 165, xi, xii
dosage
    adjustment 24, 25, 26, 27, 104, 165, xi, xii
dream interpretation 24, 25, 26, 27, 104, 165, xi, xii
drug
    prescription
    illicit
    war on 24, 25, 26, 27, 104, 165, xi, xii
duration
    regulating 24, 25, 26, 27, 104, 165, xi, xii
dysfunction
    serotonin 24, 25, 26, 27, 104, 165, xi, xii
ecstasy
    MDMA 24, 25, 26, 27, 104, 165, xi, xii
ego strength 24, 25, 26, 27, 104, 165, xi, xii
emotional
    adjustments
    obstacles
    resolution 24, 25, 26, 27, 104, 165, xi, xii
    obstacles
    debris 24, 25, 26, 27, 104, 165, xi, xii
    past
    terrain
    themes 24, 25, 26, 27, 104, 165, xi, xii
emotional pain 24, 25, 26, 27, 104, 165, xi, xii
empathy 24, 25, 26, 27, 104, 165, xi, xii
empty chair 24, 25, 26, 27, 104, 165, xi, xii
endorphins
    receptor site
    function 24, 25, 26, 27, 104, 165, xi, xii
enkaphalin 24, 25, 26, 27, 104, 165, xi, xii
essential ingredients 24, 25, 26, 27, 104, 165, xi, xii
estrogen 24, 25, 26, 27, 104, 165, xi, xii
existential theory 24, 25, 26, 27, 104, 165, xi, xii
fake identification 24, 25, 26, 27, 104, 165, xi, xii
fear
    and inner reality
    and status quo
    enacting change 24, 25, 26, 27, 104, 165, xi, xii
    past
    function of
    and foudation beliefs 24, 25, 26, 27, 104, 165, xi, xii
feedback
    mechanisms
    verbal 24, 25, 26, 27, 104, 165, xi, xii
fight flight freeze response 24, 25, 26, 27, 104, 165, xi, xii
flush 24, 25, 26, 27, 104, 165, xi, xii
flushing 24, 25, 26, 27, 104, 165,

xi, xii
foundation
    of inner reality
    learning
    esperience 24, 25, 26, 27, 104, 165, xi, xii
frequency
    of visits
    of BST use 24, 25, 26, 27, 104, 165, xi, xii
GABA
    function
    receptor sites 24, 25, 26, 27, 104, 165, xi, xii
gamma amino butyric acid 24, 25, 26, 27, 104, 165, xi, xii
gastrointestinal
    distress 24, 25, 26, 27, 104, 165, xi, xii
gatekeepers
    emotional 24, 25, 26, 27, 104, 165, xi, xii
gene expression 24, 25, 26, 27, 104, 165, xi, xii
gestalt
    therapy 24, 25, 26, 27, 104, 165, xi, xii
gifting 24, 25, 26, 27, 104, 165, xi, xii
glutamate 24, 25, 26, 27, 104, 165, xi, xii
glycine 24, 25, 26, 27, 104, 165, xi, xii
goal directed strengths perspective 24, 25, 26, 27, 104, 165, xi, xii
goldfinger method
    development of 24, 25, 26, 27, 104, 165, xi, xii
goodbye letter 24, 25, 26, 27, 104, 165, xi, xii
grief
    relationship
    and sobriety
    substance 24, 25, 26, 27, 104, 165, xi, xii
guilt 24, 25, 26, 27, 104, 165, xi, xii
hallucination 24, 25, 26, 27, 104, 165, xi, xii
hardware 24, 25, 26, 27, 104, 165, xi, xii
harm reduction
    treatment 24, 25, 26, 27, 104, 165, xi, xii
heroin 24, 25, 26, 27, 104, 165, xi, xii
hippocampus 24, 25, 26, 27, 104, 165, xi, xii
histamine 24, 25, 26, 27, 104, 165, xi, xii
holotropic breathwork 24, 25, 26, 27, 104, 165, xi, xii
hormones 24, 25, 26, 27, 104, 165, xi, xii
humor
    lens 24, 25, 26, 27, 104, 165, xi, xii
hypermnesia 24, 25, 26, 27, 104, 165, xi, xii
hyperventilation
    and anxiety treatment
    and holotropic breathwork 24, 25, 26, 27, 104, 165, xi, xii

Index

hypnosis
    for substance abuse treatment
    and ideomotor questioning 24, 25, 26, 27, 104, 165, xi, xii
hypothalamic response 24, 25, 26, 27, 104, 165, xi, xii
hypothalamus 24, 25, 26, 27, 104, 165, xi, xii
ideomotor expression 24, 25, 26, 27, 104, 165, xi, xii
ideomotor questioning
    substance state
    emotional state
    obstacles to BST 24, 25, 26, 27, 104, 165, xi, xii
ideomotor signals
    development of
    variations of 24, 25, 26, 27, 104, 165, xi, xii
ideosensory signals 24, 25, 26, 27, 104, 165, xi, xii
imbalance
    usual reality 24, 25, 26, 27, 104, 165, xi, xii
impersonators
    molecular 24, 25, 26, 27, 104, 165, xi, xii
incentive sensitization 24, 25, 26, 27, 104, 165, xi, xii
induction
    hypnotic 24, 25, 26, 27, 104, 165, xi, xii
inebriation 24, 25, 26, 27, 104, 165, xi, xii
information processing
    auditory
    visual
    kinesthetic 24, 25, 26, 27, 104, 165, xi, xii
information substance 24, 25, 26, 27, 104, 165, xi, xii
inner reality
    development of
    foundation of 24, 25, 26, 27, 104, 165, xi, xii
insulation
    experienal
    emotional 24, 25, 26, 27, 104, 165, xi, xii
intelligence
    non-conscious
    unconscious 24, 25, 26, 27, 104, 165, xi, xii
intention
    of utilization sobriety 24, 25, 26, 27, 104, 165, xi, xii
judgment
    free
    inner reality 24, 25, 26, 27, 104, 165, xi, xii
Ketamine 24, 25, 26, 27, 104, 165, xi, xii
kinesthetic
    representational system 24, 25, 26, 27, 104, 165, xi, xii
lacrimation 24, 25, 26, 27, 104, 165, xi, xii
language
    lens
    client 24, 25, 26, 27, 104, 165, xi, xii

lens
> of strengths perspective 24, 25, 26, 27, 104, 165, xi, xii

levitation
> hand 24, 25, 26, 27, 104, 165, xi, xii

ligand 24, 25, 26, 27, 104, 165, xi, xii

limbic
> system
> cortex
> emotional experience 24, 25, 26, 27, 104, 165, xi, xii

link
> anxiety and alcoholism
> body-mind
> substance abuse treatment 24, 25, 26, 27, 104, 165, xi, xii

locus of control
> internal
> external 24, 25, 26, 27, 104, 165, xi, xii

LSD 24, 25, 26, 27, 104, 165, xi, xii

maintenance 24, 25, 26, 27, 104, 165, xi, xii

marijuana 24, 25, 26, 27, 104, 165, xi, xii

maze 24, 25, 26, 27, 104, 165, xi, xii

meaning
> lens 24, 25, 26, 27, 104, 165, xi, xii

medical
> concerns

release of information coordination 24, 25, 26, 27, 104, 165, xi, xii

memory
> implicit
> socially accessible
> traumatic 24, 25, 26, 27, 104, 165, xi, xii
> types of
> functions 24, 25, 26, 27, 104, 165, xi, xii

mesolimbic dopaminergic system 24, 25, 26, 27, 104, 165, xi, xii

methadone 24, 25, 26, 27, 104, 165, xi, xii

methamphetamine 24, 25, 26, 27, 104, 165, xi, xii

milk carton 24, 25, 26, 27, 104, 165, xi, xii

motivation
> influences on
> level of 24, 25, 26, 27, 104, 165, xi, xii

motivational interviewing 24, 25, 26, 27, 104, 165, xi, xii

Mr. Clean 24, 25, 26, 27, 104, 165, xi, xii

naltrexone 24, 25, 26, 27, 104, 165, xi, xii

naming
> BST 24, 25, 26, 27, 104, 165, xi, xii

narcotics anonymous 24, 25, 26, 27, 104, 165, xi, xii

narrative therapy 24, 25, 26, 27, 104, 165, xi, xii

native dialect 24, 25, 26, 27, 104,

165, xi, xii
neurognesis 24, 25, 26, 27, 104, 165, xi, xii
neuronal network 24, 25, 26, 27, 104, 165, xi, xii
neurotransmitter 24, 25, 26, 27, 104, 165, xi, xii
nicotine 24, 25, 26, 27, 104, 165, xi, xii
noradrenaline 24, 25, 26, 27, 104, 165, xi, xii
norepinephrine
    function
    receptor site 24, 25, 26, 27, 104, 165, xi, xii
oblivion
    total 24, 25, 26, 27, 104, 165, xi, xii
obsessive-compulsive 24, 25, 26, 27, 104, 165, xi, xii
obstacles
    to BST formation
    emotional
    hierarchy of 24, 25, 26, 27, 104, 165, xi, xii
opioid
    derivatives 24, 25, 26, 27, 104, 165, xi, xii
    endogenous
    dependency
    receptor site 24, 25, 26, 27, 104, 165, xi, xii
pace
    emotional experience 24, 25, 26, 27, 104, 165, xi, xii
peptide 24, 25, 26, 27, 104, 165, xi, xii
perceptual possibility 24, 25, 26, 27, 104, 165, xi, xii
percocet 24, 25, 26, 27, 104, 165, xi, xii
personal history
    lens 24, 25, 26, 27, 104, 165, xi, xii
pharmaceutical
    solutions
    intervention
    commercials
    commercials 24, 25, 26, 27, 104, 165, xi, xii
picture change 24, 25, 26, 27, 104, 165, xi, xii
player
    physiological
    biochemical 24, 25, 26, 27, 104, 165, xi, xii
post-traumatic stress disorder
    PTSD
    and substance abuse treatment 24, 25, 26, 27, 104, 165, xi, xii
power
    perception of
    personal 24, 25, 26, 27, 104, 165, xi, xii
precontemplation 24, 25, 26, 27, 104, 165, xi, xii
preparation 24, 25, 26, 27, 104, 165, xi, xii
preposition 24, 25, 26, 27, 104, 165, xi, xii
problem
    lens 24, 25, 26, 27, 104, 165, xi, xii

process addiction 24, 25, 26, 27, 104, 165, xi, xii
procrastination 24, 25, 26, 27, 104, 165, xi, xii
progesterone 24, 25, 26, 27, 104, 165, xi, xii
pronoun 24, 25, 26, 27, 104, 165, xi, xii
protective function 24, 25, 26, 27, 104, 165, xi, xii
psycho-neuro-somato-sensory network 24, 25, 26, 27, 104, 165, xi, xii
psychodynamic
    treatment
        roadblocks 24, 25, 26, 27, 104, 165, xi, xii
puzzle 24, 25, 26, 27, 104, 165, xi, xii
rapport 24, 25, 26, 27, 104, 165, xi, xii
ratification
    of behavior
    of immediate experience
    of cognition 24, 25, 26, 27, 104, 165, xi, xii
    of imagery 24, 25, 26, 27, 104, 165, xi, xii
ratification of imagery 24, 25, 26, 27, 104, 165, xi, xii
rationalization 24, 25, 26, 27, 104, 165, xi, xii
rational emotive therapy 24, 25, 26, 27, 104, 165, xi, xii
rational recovery 24, 25, 26, 27, 104, 165, xi, xii
reframe
    naturalistic 24, 25, 26, 27, 104, 165, xi, xii
reinforcement 24, 25, 26, 27, 104, 165, xi, xii
relapse
    recovery
    prevention 24, 25, 26, 27, 104, 165, xi, xii
relationship
    dependent
    addictive
    substance 24, 25, 26, 27, 104, 165, xi, xii
representational system
    auditory
    visual
    kinesthetic 24, 25, 26, 27, 104, 165, xi, xii
resistance 24, 25, 26, 27, 104, 165, xi, xii
resolution hierarchy 24, 25, 26, 27, 104, 165, xi, xii
sabotage 24, 25, 26, 27, 104, 165, xi, xii
saccadic 24, 25, 26, 27, 104, 165, xi, xii
secular organization for sobriety 24, 25, 26, 27, 104, 165, xi, xii
seeding 24, 25, 26, 27, 104, 165, xi, xii
self-efficacy 24, 25, 26, 27, 104, 165, xi, xii
sensory
    channel
    experience
    lens 24, 25, 26, 27, 104, 165, xi, xii

serotonin
> receptor site
>> function 24, 25, 26, 27, 104, 165, xi, xii

sexual identity 24, 25, 26, 27, 104, 165, xi, xii

shame 24, 25, 26, 27, 104, 165, xi, xii

smart recovery 24, 25, 26, 27, 104, 165, xi, xii

sobriety
> establishment of
>> maintenance 24, 25, 26, 27, 104, 165, xi, xii

software 24, 25, 26, 27, 104, 165, xi, xii

solution focused approaches 24, 25, 26, 27, 104, 165, xi, xii

spirit
> lens 24, 25, 26, 27, 104, 165, xi, xii

SSRI
> selective serotonin reuptake inhibitor
>> function 24, 25, 26, 27, 104, 165, xi, xii

state
> inebriated
> benefit
>> substance 24, 25, 26, 27, 104, 165, xi, xii

state-dependent learning, memory and behavior
> accessing
> utilizing
>> theory of 24, 25, 26, 27, 104, 165, xi, xii

strengths perspective 24, 25, 26, 27, 104, 165, xi, xii

substance
> state
> use history
>> type 24, 25, 26, 27, 104, 165, xi, xii

support groups
> attendance 24, 25, 26, 27, 104, 165, xi, xii

survival
> memory 24, 25, 26, 27, 104, 165, xi, xii

team
> our
> other 24, 25, 26, 27, 104, 165, xi, xii

temporal position 24, 25, 26, 27, 104, 165, xi, xii

temporal shift 24, 25, 26, 27, 104, 165, xi, xii

termination 24, 25, 26, 27, 104, 165, xi, xii

testosterone 24, 25, 26, 27, 104, 165, xi, xii

time
> continuum
> lens
>> distortion 24, 25, 26, 27, 104, 165, xi, xii

trance phenomena 24, 25, 26, 27, 104, 165, xi, xii

transport
> neurotransmitter
>> dopamine 24, 25, 26, 27, 104, 165, xi, xii

trazodone 24, 25, 26, 27, 104,

165, xi, xii
treatment
    substance abuse
    state of substance abuse 24, 25, 26, 27, 104, 165, xi, xii
trigger
    rehearsal
    identification 24, 25, 26, 27, 104, 165, xi, xii
twitch 24, 25, 26, 27, 104, 165, xi, xii
unconscious mind
    communication with
    expression of
    language of 24, 25, 26, 27, 104, 165, xi, xii
utilization
    principle
    sobriety method 24, 25, 26, 27, 104, 165, xi, xii
utilization sobriety
    method
    intention 24, 25, 26, 27, 104, 165, xi, xii
verbs 24, 25, 26, 27, 104, 165, xi, xii
vibration 24, 25, 26, 27, 104, 165, xi, xii
visual
    representational system 24, 25, 26, 27, 104, 165, xi, xii
withdrawal
    options
    strategies 24, 25, 26, 27, 104, 165, xi, xii
women for sobriety 24, 25, 26, 27, 104, 165, xi, xii

Index